*ISBN EAN-13:*     978-1-938117-45-9     [Soft cover Print Edition]

## Golden Words Upon Golden Words...For Every Muslim.

"Imaam al-Barbahaaree, may Allaah have mercy upon him said:

**May Allaah have mercy upon you! Examine carefully the speech of everyone you hear from in your time particularly. So do not act in haste and do not enter into anything from it until you ask and see: Did any of the Companions of the Prophet, may Allaah's praise and salutations be upon him, speak about it, or did any of the scholars? So if you find a narration from them about it, cling to it, do not go beyond it for anything and do not give precedence to anything over it and thus fall into the Fire.**

Explanation by Sheikh Saaleh al-Fauzaan, may Allaah preserve him:

'Do not be hasty in accepting as correct what you may hear from the people especially in these later times. As now there are many who speak about so many various matters, issuing rulings and ascribing to themselves both knowledge and the right to speak. This is especially the case after the emergence and spread of new modern day media technologies. Such that everyone now can speak and bring forth that which is in truth worthless; by this meaning words of no true value - speaking about whatever they wish in the name of knowledge and in the name of the religion of Islaam. It has even reached the point that you find the people of misguidance and the members of the various groups of misguidance and deviance from the religion speaking as well. Such individuals have now become those who speak in the name of the religion of Islaam through means such as the various satellite television channels. Therefore be very cautious!

It is upon you oh Muslim, and upon you oh student of knowledge individually, to verify matters and not rush to embrace everything and anything you may hear. It is upon you to verify the truth of what you hear, asking, 'Who else also makes this same statement or claim?', 'Where did this thought or concept originate or come from?', 'Who is its reference or source authority?'. Asking what are the evidences which support it from within the Book and the Sunnah? And inquiring where has the individual who is putting this forth studied and taken his knowledge from? From who has he studied the knowledge of Islaam?

Each of these matters requires verification through inquiry and investigation, especially in the present age and time. As it is not every speaker who should rightly be considered a source of knowledge, even if he is well spoken and eloquent, and can manipulate words captivating his listeners. Do not be taken in and accept him until you are aware of the degree and scope of what he possesses of knowledge and understanding. As perhaps someone's words may be few, but possess true understanding, and perhaps another will have a great deal of speech yet he is actually ignorant to such a degree that he doesn't actually posses anything of true understanding. Rather he only has the ability to enchant with his speech so that the people are deceived. Yet he puts forth the perception that he is a scholar, that he is someone of true understanding and comprehension, that he is a capable thinker, and so forth. Through such means and ways he is able to deceive and beguile the people, taking them away from the way of truth.

Therefore what is to be given true consideration is not the amount of the speech put forth or that one can extensively discuss a subject. Rather the criterion that is to be given consideration is what that speech contains within it of sound authentic knowledge, what it contains of the established and transmitted principles of Islaam. As perhaps a short or brief statement which is connected to or has a foundation in the established principles can be of greater benefit than a great deal of speech which simply rambles on, and through hearing you don't actually receive very much benefit from.

This is the reality which is present in our time; one sees a tremendous amount of speech which only possesses within it a small amount of actual knowledge. We see the presence of many speakers yet few people of true understanding and comprehension.' "

*[The eminent major scholar Sheikh Saaleh al-Fauzaan, may Allaah preserve him- 'A Valued Gift for the Reader Of Comments Upon the Book Sharh as-Sunnah', page 102-103]*

*With Selections from the Following Scholars:*

**Sheikh 'Abdul-'Azeez ibn 'Abdullah ibn Baaz -Sheikh Muhammad ibn Saaleh al-'Utheimein - Sheikh Muhammad Naasiruddeen al-Albaanee - Sheikh Muqbil ibn Haadee al-Waada'ee - Sheikh 'Abdur-Rahman ibn Naaser as-Sa'adee - Sheikh Muhammad 'Amaan al-Jaamee - Sheikh Muhammad al-Ameen as-Shanqeetee - Sheikh Ahmad ibn Yahya an-Najmee**

*(May Allaah have mercy upon them.)* &

**Sheikh Saaleh al-Fauzaan ibn 'Abdullah al-Fauzaan - Sheikh Saaleh ibn 'Abdul-'Azeez Aal-Sheikh - Sheikh Muhammad ibn 'Abdul-Wahhab al-Wasaabee -Permanent Committee to Scholastic Research & Issuing Of Islamic Rulings**

*(May Allaah preserve them.)*

*With an introduction by:*
*Sheikh Muhammad Ibn 'Abdullah al-Imaam*
*Collected and Translated*
*by Abu Sukhailah Khalil Ibn-Abelahyi al-Amreekee*

[Available: **Now** pages: **370+**
price: (Soft cover) **$25**
(Hard cover) **$32**
(eBook) **$9.99**]

A TREASURY OF GUIDANCE FOR THE MUSLIM
STRIVING TO LEARN HIS RELIGION:
# SHEIKH MUQBIL IBN HAADEE AL-WAADI'EE

*Statements of the Guiding Scholars Pocket Edition 2*

*Translated & Compiled By*
Abu Sukhailah Khalil Ibn-Abelahyi al-Amreekee

# Table of Contents

(50)  Question: Along with the many people who verify the books
from our righteous predecessors in this age; there are some verifiers
who initially brought forth books in which are found beneficial points
regarding general knowledge and correct belief. Then after they became
well known among the ranks of youth, they began to bring forth
strange statements and inconsistencies. How can the youth deal with
this situation where there is little or no warning from the scholars
regarding these shortcomings? From these verifiers, as an example, is
the Sheikh 'Abdul-Qaadir al-Arnaa'out and his verification of 'Aqaawel
at-Thiqaat' of Karemee. We benefit from his introduction in relation
to issues of correct belief and his refutation the distortion of the source
texts by Asha'ree sect. However in contrast to this, in his comments
within 'Saheeh Ibn Hibbaan', he brings forth similar distortions as
them of some attributes of Allaah and legitimizes it. So we hope for a
warning from these errors, and that you clarify for us the condition and
level of some of the authors and verifiers in our time.........................250

# Images of handwritten original introduction of Sheikh Muhammad Ibn 'Abdullah al-Imaam (may Allaah preserve him)

بسم الله الرحمن الرحيم

**دار الحديث للعلوم الشرعية**
**محمد بن عبدالله الإمام**

التاريخ ١٨ / ٣ / ١٤٢٥هـ

الحمد لله والصلاة والسلام على رسول الله وعلى آله وصحبه

أما بعد

لقد اطلعني الأخ / خليل بهرا بيلا هي حفظه الله
على ما قام به من جمع كلام بعض اهل العلم في الكتب
التي ينصح المسلم بقراءتها والكتب التي كذ رالمسلم
من قراءتها قراءته فقد جمع جمعاطلها هيرا هل العلم
فنا اسم المسؤول أن ينفع بذلك وهذا من فضل الله
على اصحبنا الفاضل المذكور وأعلا ان يكون والاعلا
الكبير مقتفيا بالرسول صلى الله عليهم وسلم دمسا واعلا بخير
فلم مثل اجرفا عليا

اليمن - لواء ذمار - معبر - هاتف : ٤٣٠٥٢١ - تلفاكس : ٤٣٠٢٨٠ - ص . ب : ٨٦٠٠١

# Images of handwritten original introduction of Sheikh Muhammad Ibn 'Abdullah al-Imaam (may Allaah preserve him)

## Introduction of Sheikh Muhammad Ibn 'Abdullah al-Imaam (may Allaah preserve him)

All praise is due to Allaah, may Allaah's praise and His salutations be upon the Messenger of Allaah, his family, and Companions.

As for what follows:

The brother Khalil Ibn-Abelahyi, may Allaah preserve him, has shown to me that which he has undertaken in gathering the speech of some of the people of knowledge regarding the books the Muslims are advised to read, as well as those books that the Muslims are warned against reading.

After reading it, I see that he has compiled a collection from the statements of well-known people of knowledge, and he has selected well and brought forth good for the Muslims in what he presents to them in this blessed book. How can this not be so, when the foundation of every good is in reading the book that possesses benefit and in having a righteous teacher? As the scholars have mentioned, *"The one who carefully selects his teacher and his book has protected his religion with the best of safeguards."*

Sheikh Ibn al-'Utheimeen, may Allaah have mercy upon him, was asked, "At whose hands should we take knowledge?" He replied, *"From the one of correct beliefs, sound methodology, and the proper goal and objective."* Likewise, the author of the 'Risaa'il al-Islaah' stated, *"The rectification of the Muslim nation is through the correction of its deeds and endeavors, and the correction of its deeds and endeavors is based upon the rectification of its branches of knowledge, and the rectification of its branches of knowledge lies in the reliable transmitters of its knowledge.*" Consider what Ibn Taymeeyah has said regarding Abee Haamed al-Ghazaalee: "*The book ash-Shifaa' caused him to become afflicted...*" (Majmu'a al-Fatawaa, Vol. 10, Page 552). Meaning that the illness of Abu Haamed originated from the reading and studying the book ash-Shifaa' of Ibn Sinaa, due to what it contains of deviations that lead one outside of Islaam. May Allaah be generous to the one who said:

> *We ceased our brotherhood with those*
> > *who became diseased from the Book Ash-Shifaa'*
> *And how many times have I said, oh people you are*
> > *on the very edge of the cliff because of the book*
> > *Ash- Shifaa' '*
> *When they dismissed our warning to them*
> > *we return in death, back to Allaah with Him being*
> > *sufficient for us,*
> *Yet they then died upon the religion of Ibn Rustaalas!*
> > *while we lived upon the way of the chosen Messenger.*

(Majmu'a al-Fatawaa, Vol. 9, Page 253)

Therefore from the completeness of a Muslim's protection from harm and trials is that he does not acquire a book or choose it for reading or study until he inquires about that book from someone whom he knows is reliable in both his religion and his knowledge.

How many diseases of our Muslim nation are caused by reading books that are not truly reliable when judging according to the guidance of the Sharee'ah! Therefore as a statement of ample warning regarding every book in which its harm is known to be greater than its good, it is not permissible to publish it, read it, or give it as a gift.

As for the books of the sects of the Raafidhah, the Sufeeyah, the people of philosophical argument and false rhetoric- then it should be known assuredly that their evil and harm is significantly greater than any good within them. So from the completeness of a Muslim's protecting himself from harm and trials is that he does not acquire a book or choose it for reading or study until he inquires about that book from someone whom he knows is reliable regarding his religion and knowledge.

Written by
Muhammad Ibn 'Abdullah al-Imaam

# Compiler's Introduction (Pocket Edition)

*In the name of Allaah, The Most Gracious, The Most Merciful*

Verily, all praise is due to Allaah, we praise Him, we seek His assistance and we ask for His forgiveness. We seek refuge in Him from the evils of our souls and the evils of our actions. Whoever Allaah guides, no one can lead him astray and whoever is caused to go astray, there is no one that can guide him. I bear witness that there is no deity worthy of worship except Allaah alone with no partners. And I bear witness that Muhammad is His worshipper and Messenger.

❝ *Oh you who believe, fear Allaah as He ought to be feared and do not die except while you are Muslims.* ❞ -(Surah Aal-'Imraan:102)

❝ *Oh mankind, fear Allaah who created you from a single soul and from that, He created its mate. And from them He brought forth many men and women. And fear Allaah to whom you demand your mutual rights. Verily, Allaah is an ever All-Watcher over you.* ❞ -(Surah an-Nisaa:1)

❝ *Oh you who believe, fear Allaah and speak a word that is truthful (and to the point) - He will rectify your deeds and forgive you your sins. And whoever obeys Allaah and His Messenger has achieved a great success.* ❞ -(Surah al-Ahzaab:70-71)

As for what follows:

The best speech is the book of Allaah, and the best guidance is the guidance of Muhammad, may Allaah's praise and His salutations be upon him. And the worst of affairs are newly invented matters in the religion, and every newly invented matter in an innovation, and every innovation is a going astray, and every going astray is in the Fire.

Certainly, every Muslim hopes for success and happiness in this world and the Hereafter. Our Lord has taught us to ask Him for guidance in the "Mother" of al-Qur'aan, Surah al-Faatihah, where He explains to us exactly which path is the true path to contentment and the true way of success. The guiding scholar Sheikh 'Abdul-'Azeez Ibn 'Abdullah Ibn Baaz, may Allaah have mercy upon him, comprehensively described this path to happiness:

*"...the path to happiness and the path to success is the path which was taken by the first believers, the Companions of the Prophet, may Allaah's praise and His salutations be upon him, and those who followed them in goodness. As Allaah, the Majestic and the Exalted, says,* ❧ *... **this is my straight path. Follow it and do not follow the other paths as they will separate you from His path. This is what he has ordained for you, in order that you may become righteous.*** ❧ *–(Surah al-Anaam: 153) The path of Allaah is knowledge, this truly is His path, this truly is guidance, this truly is Islaam, this truly is goodness, and this truly is the fear of Allaah.*

*Regarding this, Allaah, Glorified and Exalted, says in Surah al-Faatihah,* ❧ ***Guide us to the straight path.*** ❧ *Our Lord has instructed us to ask for this; instructed that we ask from Him guidance to His straight path. And His straight path is that knowledge that was brought by His Messenger, as well as acting according to that."* [1]

The hadeeth scholar Sheikh Hamaad Ibn al-Ansaaree, may Allaah have mercy upon him, explained the meaning this verse, ❧ ***Guide us to the straight path*** ❧ which is recited by all of us in our ritual prayers:

---

[1]    From our sheikh's comments upon "Understanding of the Religion' by Sheikh Saaleh al-Fauzaan

*"The meaning of ◈ Guide us to the straight path ◈ is: Our Lord whom we have praised by means of what You have taught us. We ask You and supplicate to You by this supplication, which You have taught us, that You guide us to the straight path. And the meaning of ◈ Guide us to the straight path ◈ is: Teach us that which will benefit us, and then grant us success to act in accordance with that which benefits us.'"* [2]

Indeed, from the greatest means to achieving this foundation of success and happiness; is the seeking of beneficial knowledge and acting according to it. As was mentioned by Sheikh al-Islaam Ibn Taymeeyah, may Allaah have mercy upon him:

*"The seeking of Sharee'ah knowledge is generally a communal obligation upon the Muslims together collectively, except for that which has been specified as an obligation for each and every individual. For example, the seeking of knowledge of what Allaah has commanded everyone in general and what He has forbidden for them. The obtainment of that type of knowledge is considered an obligation upon every individual. As it has been narrated in the two 'Saheeh' collections from the Prophet, may Allaah's praise and His salutations be upon him, that he said, {The one whom Allaah intends good for He gives him understanding of his religion.}"* [3] [4]

---

[2]    Risaa'il feel-Aqeedah: page 22

[3]    This hadeeth {*The one whom Allaah intends…*} is found in Saheeh al-Bukhaaree: 71, 3116, 7312/ Saheeh Muslim: 1037/ Sunan Ibn Maajah: 221/ al-Muwatta Maalik: 1300, 1667/ Musnad Imaam Ahmad: 16395, 16404, and other narrations/ Musannaf Ibn Abee Shaaybah: 31792/ & Sunan al-Daramee: 224, 226/- on the authority of Mu'aweeyah. And it is found in Jaame' al-Tirmidhee: 2645/ Musnad Imaam Ahmad: 2786/ & Sunan ad-Daaramee: 270, 2706/- on the authority of Ibn Abbaas. And  it is found in Sunan Ibn Maajah: 220/ & Musannaf 'Abdul-Razzaaq: 30851/- on the authority of Abee Hurairah. It was declared authentic by Sheikh al-Albanee in Saheeh al-Aadab al-Mufrad: 517, Silsilat al-Hadeeth as-Saheehah: 1194, 1195, 1196, Saheeh at-Targheeb at-Tarheeb: 67, as well as in other of his books. Sheikh Muqbil declared it authentic in al-Jaame' al-Saheeh: 9, 3123, 4650, may Allaah have mercy upon them both

[4]    Majmu'a al-Fatawaa: vol. 28/80

The guiding scholar Sheikh Ibn Baaz, may Allaah have mercy upon him, explained the meaning of "Sharee'ah" knowledge:

*"Knowledge is known to possess many merits. Certainly the noblest field of knowledge which the seekers can strive towards, and those who aspire can endeavor to reach, is gaining Sharee'ah knowledge. While the term 'knowledge' is used generally to refer to many things, within the statements of the scholars of Islaam what is intended by 'knowledge' is Sharee'ah knowledge. This is the meaning of knowledge in its general usage as expressed in the Book of Allaah and in the texts of the Sunnah of His Messenger, may Allaah's praise and His salutations be upon him. This is knowledge of Allaah and His names and attributes, knowledge of His right over those He created, and of what commands He legislated for them, Glorified and Exalted is He. It is knowledge of the true way and path, that which leads and directs toward Him, as well as its specific details. It is knowledge of the final state and destination in the next life of all those beings He created. This is Sharee'ah knowledge, and it is the highest type of knowledge. It is worthy of being sought after and its achievement should be aspired to.*

*Through this knowledge one understands who Allaah, Glorified and Exalted, is, and by means of it you are able to worship Him. Through this knowledge you understand what Allaah has permitted and what He has prohibited, what He is pleased with and what He is displeased with. And through this knowledge you understand the destiny of this life and its inevitable conclusion. That being that a group of the people will end in Paradise, achieving happiness, and the rest of the people, who are indeed the majority, will end in Hellfire, the abode of disgrace and misery."* [5]

[5]    From a lecture given by the eminent scholar at the Islamic University in Medinah on 3/26/1404

Therefore, it becomes clear that this desired goal which leads to true success, as has been mentioned, is only possible through the seeking of beneficial knowledge, meaning Sharee'ah knowledge, from its carriers- the scholars. Similarly, what is meant by the term 'scholars' are those people of knowledge from the saved and victorious group of Muslims who have always remained upon the guidance of the Messenger, may Allaah's praise and His salutations be upon him and his Companions, inwardly and outwardly, in every generation and age. They are the people of true guidance, the well-grounded scholars of Ahlus-Sunnah wa al-Jama'ah from the early generations, the later generations, and our present day scholars.

We must recognize them and affirm their position, defend their honor, and strive to assist and cooperate with them because they carry and preserve the inheritance of the Messenger of Allaah, may Allaah's praise and salutations be upon him. Sheikh al-Islaam Ibn Taymeeyah mentioned in his book, '*Lifting the Blame*', Page 10:

> "*It is obligatory upon the Muslims after loyalty to Allaah the Exalted and His Messenger, to have loyalty to the believers, as is mentioned in the Qur'aan. This is especially true in regard to the scholars, as they are the inheritors of the prophets and are those who have been placed in a position by Allaah like the stars by which we are guided through the darkness of land and sea.*
>
> *The Muslims are in consensus regarding their guidance and knowledge. Since in every nation before the sending of our Prophet Muhammad, may Allaah's praise and His salutations be upon him, their scholars were indeed the worst of their people, until the time of the Muslim Ummah; as certainly the scholars of the Muslims are the best of them. They are the successors of the Messenger, may Allaah's praise and His salutations be upon him, in his nation, and they give life to that which has died from his Sunnah...*"

It is necessary that every Muslim understand the importance of the role of the scholars and their position in our lives, being connected to them, and listening to their advice and guidance. Thereafter, it is upon us to maintain as strong connection and relationship to them as possible. Additionally, it is necessary for us to be aware of the deception, delusions, and falsehoods of those who strive to separate or distance the Muslims from our scholars, specifically coming from those people of division and group partisanship who falsely accuse the scholars of not understanding the current situation of the world, among their other false claims. They are the ones who fail to give the scholars their proper position among the people nor acknowledge their rights upon the people. The guiding scholar Saaleh al-Fauzaan, may Allaah preserve him, stated in his book, '*The Obligation of Confirming Affairs and Honoring the Scholars and an Explanation of their Position in this Ummah*' (Page 45):

> "*Specifically, we hear this in our time and age from those who speak attacking their honor and who falsely accuse the scholars of ignorance, short-sightedness and a lack of understanding of current affairs, as they claim; and this is a very dangerous matter. Because if we are deprived of the reliable ones from the Muslim scholars, who will lead the Muslim Ummah? Who will be turned to for rulings and judgments?*

> *And I believe this to be a devised plan from our enemies. This is a plan which has deceived many who do not properly understand matters and those who do possess an intense love and strong enthusiasm for Islaam, but which is only based upon ignorance. So they have intense love and strong enthusiasm for Islaam, but the matter is not that simple. Since the most highly honored position in this Ummah is that of the scholars. It is not permitted to disparage them or accuse them of ignorance and short-sightedness, or with*

*seeking the pleasure of the rulers or to describe them as the 'scholars of the rulers' or other such descriptions. This is extremely dangerous, oh worshiper of Allaah! So let us fear Allaah in regard to this matter and take caution. Clearly, it is as the poet said,*

*Oh scholars of the religion, oh 'salt' of the land,*

*What will rectify our affair, if the 'salt' itself is corrupt?'*
"

Therefore this connection and relationship between the Muslim and the scholar is a necessity for every Muslim and especially for the beginning student of knowledge. The esteemed major scholar Sheikh Muqbil Ibn Haadee al-Waadiee, may Allaah have mercy on him, stated in *'Tuhfat al-Mujeeb 'alaa Asilaat al-Hadhar wa Ghareeb'* (Page 181-182):

*"...So the cure is in returning to the Book of Allaah and the Sunnah of the Messenger of Allaah, may Allaah's praise and His salutations be upon him and his household, and then by returning to the scholars. As Allaah says,* ❨ **And when there came to them a matter concerning (public) security or fear, they announced it to the people. But if only they had referred it back to the Messenger or to those charged with authority amongst them, those who have the ability to derive a proper conclusion from it would have understood it.** ❩*-(Surah an-Nisaa:83) Therefore it is an obligation upon us to turn to the scholars in our affairs:* ❨**These are the parables that We send forth to the people, yet no one (truly) understands them except those with knowledge.'** ❩*-(Surah al-'Ankaboot: 43)*

*But what you see is some of the people merely memorizing three or four subjects and then taking that to the masjids, thrusting themselves forward and confronting others. Then his companions designate him 'Sheikh al-Islaam'! Is this to be considered knowledge?!?*

*Rather, the matter of knowledge is sitting upon a mat with
your legs beneath you, being patient with the necessary
hunger and poverty that comes with seeking knowledge.
Consider the state of the Companions of the Messenger of
Allaah, may Allaah's praise and His salutations be upon
him and his household, and what they were patient in the
face of.*

*In addition, the people of knowledge- they are the ones
who put matters in their proper places, as established
in the previous noble verse where Allaah, the One free
from imperfection and Exalted says,* ❦ **Verily, in that is a
reminder to those who possess knowledge.** ❧ *-(Surah ar-
Room: 22)'"*

In summarizing what has been mentioned of the
importance of this relationship between the worshippers of
Allaah and the guiding scholars, the major scholar Sheikh
al-Fauzaan, may Allaah preserve him, said in his book,
'*Explanation of the Mistakes of Some Authors*' (Page 18):

*"Oh Muslim youth! Oh students of knowledge! Connect
yourselves to your scholars, attach yourselves to them, and
take knowledge from them. Attach yourselves to the reliable
scholars well known for the correctness of their beliefs and
the soundness of their methodology, in order that you may
take knowledge from them and establish your connection
with your Prophet, may Allaah's praise and His salutations
be upon him, as your pious predecessors did. The Muslims
have never ceased receiving this knowledge from their
Prophet, through their scholars, generation after every
generation."*

And if one were to ask: "Who are the reliable well-known scholars?' meaning by this those well grounded in knowledge? Imaam Ibn-Qayyim, may Allaah have mercy upon him, stated:

*"The one who is well grounded in knowledge; if he is confronted with uncertain matters as numerous as the waves of the ocean, his certainty and steadfastness is not affected nor diminished, nor is he afflicted by doubt. As he is steadfast and well grounded in his knowledge, he is not disturbed by such uncertainties and doubts. Rather, what occurs with one such as this is in fact the repulsion of doubts due to his being safeguarded by his knowledge and the disturbances are thus bound and subdued...."* [6]

Certainly, Allaah facilitated for me the compilation of some of the statements of advice from the scholars regarding seeking knowledge and beneficial books, as well as their warnings against books containing misguidance. Initially, this was simply to remove ignorance from myself and the members of my family, and then afterwards also for my brothers and sisters who are also seeking knowledge. This is in order that we all are able to strive to proceed with correct methods and manners in our seeking of beneficial knowledge. This was accomplished only with the assistance of Allaah, the Most Generous.

I ask Allaah the Majestic to make this effort purely for His sake, and to accept it from me. I hope that this will be a beneficial book in this subject and area, for the one who seeks adherence to the religion of truth through the learning of beneficial knowledge -wherever they may be in the world. As was mentioned by Sheikh al-Islaam Ibn Taymeeyah, may Allaah the Exalted have mercy upon him, understanding the nature and source of beneficial knowledge is essential to obtaining it:

---

[6]    Miftah Dar as-Sa'dah: vol. 1 page 442

*"...As for which books can be utilized and relied upon in the various areas of knowledge, then this is an extensive matter. Additionally, this differs according to the differences among the young people within a certain land. Since what has been made easy for them in some lands, from knowledge, its path, and its study; has not been made possible for others in different lands. But, gather whatever goodness is possible by turning to Allaah, the Most Perfect, for assistance in acquiring the transmitted knowledge from the Prophet, may Allaah's praise and salutations be upon him. As this is what is truly entitled to be called knowledge.*

*As for other matters besides that, either it is knowledge but it is not truly beneficial, or that which is not actually knowledge but only mistakenly considered to be. Indeed if it actually was beneficial knowledge, then undoubtedly it must be from that which springs from the inherited guidance of Muhammad, may Allaah's praise and salutations be upon him. As there is nothing that can serve in its place as an alternative or substitute, from that which is considered similar to it or seen by some to be better than it.*

*Therefore, if his purpose and intent is to understand the goals and objectives of the Messenger of Allaah within everything that he commanded and that which he forbade, as well as in the rest of the Messenger's statements; and if his heart becomes satisfied with this understanding and the explanation of the rulings, this is the aim and objective of the Messenger's guidance. ...It is not possible to set straight or rectify the relationship between him and Allaah, the Most High as well as the relationship between him and the people, until he is capable of possessing this understanding. So struggle in every area of the various areas of knowledge to adhere to the foundation and fundamental knowledge which is transmitted directly from the Prophet, may Allaah's praise and salutations be upon him"* [7]

---

[7] Majmu'a al-Fatawaa: Vol. 19, page 119

## *Guide to the Symbols for Different Types of Texts or Citations Used with the Book*

❖ ❖- (...) indicates a verse of the Qur'aan and the source surah of that verse.

{...}-(...) indicates a narration of the Messenger of Allaah, may Allaah's praise and salutations be upon him, or a narration from one of the first generations or one of the scholars.

The second set of brackets -(...) is where I have in a basic format referenced and indicated some but not all, of its sources as well as its similar supporting narrations, as many times these were not present in the original printed or audio sources. All stated rulings of authenticity are from Imaam al-Albaanee or Imaam Muqbil, may Allaah have mercy upon both of them, according to my limited ability. Similarly I have sometimes mentioned other relevant statements about the referred to narrations from these two distinguished scholars which I found in their books. Lastly, long source citations according to narrator have been separated from the text as numbered footnotes to facilitate reading. It should also be noted that the numbering systems of editions vary widely, and in newer printed or electronic editions the enumeration may differ.

[...] indicates an incorrect statement found among some of the common people or from the callers to falsehood whether from a book or tape.

In this text I have translated the original Arabic expression which is transliterated as, *'salla Allaahu aleihi wa sallam'* in reference to the Messenger of Allaah Muhammad Ibn 'Abdullah, according to the explanation found with the scholars of Ahlus-Sunnah wa al-Jama'ah. Its' meaning is explained in the compilation *'Salafee Selections from the Explanation of Aqeedah al-Waasiteeyah'*. Sheikh al-'Utheimeen, may Allaah the Most High have mercy upon him, stated on pages 114-115,

> *"As for the meaning of "salla Allaahu aleihi" the most accurate of what has been stated regarding this is what has been related from Abu Aleeyah, may Allaah have mercy upon him: 'It is Allaah's praise and commendation of him among the highest gatherings and assemblies in the heavens.'*

> *...And as for the meaning of "sallam" for him, within it is a statement of his being preserved from errors and shortcomings, and in the statement of "salat" upon him is an affirmation of his realization of the good characteristics and traits... So the single sentence with: "salat' and "sallam' contains an expression that informs but whose meaning is in fact one of asking or requesting by the speaker, as what is intended is supplication to Allaah.'*

Sheikh al-Fauzaan, may Allaah preserve, commented on page 116 of that same work:

> *"And the statement "salla Allaahu aleihi" linguistically carried the meaning of supplication; and the most authentic of what has been stated regarding the meaning of the "salat" from Allaah upon His Messenger is what Imaam al-Bukhaaree mentions in his Saheeh collection from Abu 'Aleeyah that he said: 'It is Allaah's praise and commendation of him among the highest gatherings and assemblies in the heavens.'... and the "sallam" means: salutations of honor or mention of his soundness and freedom from faults and failings'*

Therefore within this book its most common transliterated form, "*salla Allaahu aleihi wa sallam*" has been translated as: may Allaah's praise and salutations be upon him, and "*salla Allaahu aleihi wa alaa ahlehe wa sallam*" has been translated as: "may Allaah's praise and salutations be upon him and his household'.

## Words of Thanks and Appreciation

I thank Allaah, Glorified and Exalted, for every blessing He has given me. I ask for good mention and prayers and blessings be upon the Prophet of mercy and the Messenger of guidance Muhammad and his family. I wish to thank our esteemed Sheikh Abu Nasr Muhammad Ibn 'Abdullah al-Imaam, may Allaah preserve him, as I occupied his valuable time on more than one occasion, seeking his assistance in the affairs of my deen....

I ask Allaah, Glorified and Exalted, to place me and every Muslim and Muslimah upon the path of beneficial knowledge and righteous actions, and to enable us to walk in the truly successful path as our pious predecessors did so that our knowledge a proof for us and not against us. May Allaah's praise and His salutations be upon our Prophet Muhammad and upon his family and Companions, and all those who follow his guidance until the Day of Judgment. And all praise is due to Allaah, Lord of the Worlds.

*Written by Abu Sukhailah*
*Khalil Ibn-Abelahyi al-Amreekee*

*(Abridged for Pocket Edition)*

# (1)

Y ADVICE
To THE YOUTH OF
THE REVIVAL OF
ISLAAM

What is considered the present Islamic revival in this age should in reality be considered a sign from the signs or proofs of the truth of the Messenger's prophethood, as its presence is despite the fact that the conditions of our age have weakened the efforts of those who truly call to Allaah. And from those affairs which in the recent past have harmed and greatly diminished the efforts towards implementing Islaam are:

1- Wars and internal conflicts among the Muslims within their lands.

2- The neglect of the rulers of the Muslims to give priority and true importance to Islaam.

3- The occupation of many of the scholars and the Muslims with worldly gains; and their preoccupation with this rather than true concern for knowledge and teaching.

4- Dangerous ideological trends originating from the enemies of Islaam which are directed towards us, and which turn people away from the religion and belittle those who hold steadfastly to it, asserting that they are people who wish to return to the past and are backwards. Allaah alone frustrated their aspirations and made their deceptions and plans ineffective and fruitless, as the hearts of the Muslims are accepting Islaam and turning more towards Islaam and acknowledging the guidance of our Prophet Muhammad, may Allaah's praise and His salutations be upon him and upon his family.

In view of this one may recall that which is narrated by Imaam al-Bukhaaree where he mentioned that Abdullah Ibn Abee al-Aswad narrated to us, that Yahya informed us from Isma'eel, that Qais narrated to us that he heard al-Mugheerah Ibn Shu'ba say: I heard the Messenger of Allaah, may Allaah's praise and salutations be upon us, say,

*{A group of my Ummah will remain victorious until Allaah's Order (the Hour) comes upon them while they are still predominant victorious.}* [1]. And Imaam al-Bukhaaree, may Allaah have mercy upon him, also mentioned that al-Humaidee narrated to us, that al-Waleed narrated to us, saying: Ibn Jaabir narrated to me saying, Umair Ibn Haanee narrated to me that he heard Mu'aweeyah say: I heard the Prophet, upon him and his household be Allaah's praises and the best of salutations, saying, *{A group of my Ummah will keep on following Allaah's Laws strictly and they will not be harmed by those who will abandon them nor by those who stand against them until Allaah's Order (The Hour) will come while they will be in that state...}* [2]. *Umair said: Maalik Ibn Yukhamer said: Muadh said: And they are in Shaam. And Mu'aweeyah said: Maalik asserts that he heard Muadh say: They are in Shaam (the land directly north of the Arabian peninsula).*

This hadeeth is also narrated by Imaam Muslim and narrated from a group of the Companions, may Allaah be pleased with them. From them is Imraan Ibn Hussein, whose narration is found in the collection 'Sunan Abu Dawud', with a chain of narration that conforms with the conditions of Imaam Muslim, as well as the narrations of Thawbaan, Jaabir Ibn Samara, Jaabir Ibn 'Abdullah, and Abdullah Ibn 'Amr Ibn 'Aas found in 'Saheeh Muslim'. Also the hadeeth of Qirat Ibn Eyaas in 'Sunan at-Tirmidhee' regarding which Imaam Tirmidhee says, "*This hadeeth is hasan saheeh*". And from them is the narration of Salama Ibn Nufeel as-Sakuunee found in the Musnad of Imaam Ahmad and the book 'at-Tareekh' of Imaam al-Bukhaaree.

[1] Narrated in Saheeh al-Bukhaaree: 3640, 7311, 7459/ Saheeh Muslim: 1921/ & Musnad Ahmad: 17779, 17701/ -from the hadeeth of Mugheerah. Declared authentic by Sheikh al-Albaanee in Silsilaul-Hadeeth Saheehah: 1955, and by Sheikh Muqbil in al-Jaame' as-Saheeh: 4, 528, 2385, 3358.

[2] Narrated in Saheeh al-Bukhaaree: 3641, 7460/ Saheeh Muslim: 1037/ & Musnad Ahmad: 16485 -from the hadeeth of Mu'aweeyah, and in Saheeh Muslim: 1920/ & Musnad Ahmad: 21897 -from the hadeeth of Thawbaan Ibn Bejjaded. And in Jaame' al-Tirmidhee: 2192/ Sunan Ibn Maajah:6/ & Musnad Imaam Ahmad: 19849 -from the hadeeth of Qurra Ibn Eyaas. It was Declared authentic by Sheikh al-Albaanee in Silsilaul-Hadeeth Saheehah: 1957, and by Sheikh Muqbil in al-Jaame' as-Saheeh: 2384.

I have mentioned these in their entirety with their chains of narration in my book *((as-Saheeh al-Musnad min ad-Dalaa'il an-Nabuwwah)06-44)* and all praise is due to Allaah.

As for my advice to the youth of the Islamic revival than I have mentioned that within my book, *((al-Makhraaj min al-Fitnah)11-21)*, and I will summarize it here and supplement it as is necessary.

1- To have fear of Allaah. Allaah, the Most Perfect and the Most High says: ❦ *Oh you who believe! If you obey and fear Allaah, He will grant you a criterion to judge between right and wrong, or a way for you to get out from every difficulty, and will expiate for you your sins...* ❧ -(Surah al-Anfaal:29).

2- To consider every Muslim upon the earth your brother, and to direct your enmity towards the one who truly merits it- the enemies of Allaah from the Jews, the Christians, the Communists, the Ba'athists - anyone who strives to obstruct from the path of calling to Islaam. Be wary of becoming someone constrained and shackled to the leaders of one of the various groups or affiliating yourself with one group restrictedly, as Allaah, the Most High and the Most Exalted, says, ❦ *The believers are nothing else than brothers ...* ❧ -(Surah al-Hujaraat: 10) and He says, ❦ *And hold fast, all of you together, to the Rope of Allaah (i.e. this Qur'ân), and be not divided among yourselves...* ❧ -(Surah *Aal-'Imraan*:103). and He says: ❦ *And do not dispute (with one another) lest you lose courage and your strength depart...* ❧ -(Surah al-Anfaal:46). And Allaah mentions the state that may arise in which conflict and differing occur, saying, ❦ *And in whatsoever you differ, the decision thereof is with Allaah...* ❧ -(Surah al-Shura: 10) and He said, ❦ *(And) if you differ in anything amongst yourselves, refer it to Allaah and His Messenger, if you believe in Allaah and in the Last Day...* ❧ -(Surah an-Nisa:59)

3- To seriously strive towards uniting the Muslims under one leader who will have the characteristic of being from the Quraish. As the Prophet, may Allaah's praise and His salutations be upon him and his household, said, *{Our leaders are from the Quraish}* [3]. al-Haafidh Ibn Hajr in his commentary, 'Fath al-Baaree', stated, "*This has been narrated from the Prophet, may Allaah's praise and His salutations be upon him and his household, from approximately forty Companions.*" In addition, he should be from the people of the Sunnah, as the sect of the Raafidhah are from those with the greatest enmity towards Islaam, and the Shee'ah are the most ignorant of the people of Islaam. It is not suitable to have someone from an ignorant or foolish group lead and guide the Muslim Ummah. What good could possibly be found with those who say, [Being occupied by the communists is preferable to us than being dominated by the Wahaabees.]?? And they label as "Wahaabees" anyone who calls to the book of Allaah and the Sunnah of the Messenger of Allaah, may Allaah's praise and His salutations be upon him and his household. All praise is due to Allaah, now these Raafidhah here are like the dead to us; unknown and extinguished in Yemen as people claiming Islaam. The call to the Sunnah through the works *((A Garden of Paradise in Refutation of the Enemies of the Sunnah)11-18), ((The Guidance Regarding the Fading of the Tribulation from the Extremist Worshipers from the Rawaafidh in Yemen)11-17)*, and *((The Disbelief of Khomaynee in the Land of the Two Holy Sanctuaries)11-19)* exposed them. And all praise is due to Allaah, all of these books have been printed. These finished off their insignificant existence, and I watched over and oversaw this destruction. And the thanks for this is to Allaah alone.

[3]    Narrated in Musnad Ahmad: 11898/ -from the hadeeth of 'Anas Ibn Maalik. It was Declared authentic by Sheikh al-Albaanee in Irwa' al-Ghaleel :520, Saheeh at-Targheeb wa at-Tarheeb:2188, and in his comments upon hadeeth number 784 in Silsilatul-Hadeeth Saheehah he states: " '*Our leaders are from the Quraish...*' *this is a continuously narrated hadeeth of the highest level of authenticity, as was mentioned by al-Haafidh Ibn Hajr.*".

4- To open the door for jihaad in the path of Allaah; as Allaah, the Most Perfect and the Most High says, *And fight them until there is no more fitnah (disbelief and worshipping of others along with Allaah) and (all and every kind of) worship is for Allaah (Alone).*-(Surah al-Baqarah:193) and in the hadeeth of Ibn Umar on the Prophet, may Allaah's praise and His salutations be upon him and his household, *{If you engage in 'Enaah' and hold onto the tails of cows, becoming pleased with agriculture, and so abandoning jihaad, then Allaah will place a disgrace upon you that will not be raised until you return to your religion}* [4]. Jihaad in the path of Allaah is struggling against the disbelievers until the word of Allaah becomes supreme above all others. However, the majority of the fighting today is between the Muslim rulers simply for the sake of positions of worldly power, even though it is not permissible for the Muslim to fight his brother for the aim of seizing the position of leadership held by so-and-so; indeed your most valuable resource is your own life! How excellent is the one who said,

*I will never kill a man who prays*

> *for the sake of another ruler of the Quraish*

*Upon the ruler is the accountability for his authority and upon me is my own sin.*

> *We seek refuge in Allaah from ignorance and recklessness*

*Do you wish me to kill a Muslim who has committed no crime?*

> *Surely, never in my lifetime will that bring me any benefit .*

---

[4] Narrated in Sunan Abu Dawud: 3462/ & Musnad Ahmad:  4810, 4987 -from the hadeeth of 'Abdullah Ibn 'Umar. It was Declared authentic by Sheikh al-Albaanee in Silsilatul-Hadeeth Saheehah :11, in Saheeh at-Targheeb wa al-Tarheeb: 1389, as well as in other of his works.

5- That you restrict yourself to only acting upon evidence from the Book of Allaah or from the authentic Sunnah of the Messenger of Allaah, may Allaah's praise and His salutations be upon him and his household, as found in the statement of Allaah, Glorified and Exalted, *Follow what has been sent down unto you from your Lord, and follow not any Auliyaa' besides Him (Allaah). Little do you remember!*-(Surah al-'Araaf: 3) and the statement of the Most High *Whatsoever the Messenger (Muhammad) gives you, take it, and whatsoever he forbids you, abstain (from it)...*-(Surah al-Hasr: 7)

6- That you abandon revolting against the rulers and authorities except in the case of witnessing from them open and indisputable disbelief regarding which you have a clear proof from Allaah, as is mentioned in the hadeeth of 'Ubaidah which is found in both the collections of Imaam Bukharee and Imaam Muslim. This is in view of the consequences that generally result from revolting against them such as triggering and instigating severe trials and the killing of innocent people. Allaah, the Most Perfect and the Most High, says, *And whoever kills a believer intentionally, his recompense is Hell to abide therein, and the Wrath and the Curse of Allaah are upon him, and a great punishment is prepared for him.*-(Surah an-Nisaa:93). And the hadeeth of Abee Bakara, may Allaah be pleased with him, also found in the two well known 'Saheeh' collections wherein he says, *{I heard Allaah's Prophet saying, 'If two Muslims meet each other with their swords then (both) the killer and the killed one are in the HellFire.}* [5].

---

[5]    Narrated in Saheeh al-Bukhaaree: 31, 6975/ Saheeh Muslim: 2888/ Sunan Abu Dawud: 4268/ Sunan an-Nasaa'ee: 4125, 4126, 4127, 4128, 4129/ & Musnad Ahmad: 19926, 19959, 19980/ -from the hadeeth of Abu Bakrah. And in Sunan an-Nasaa'ee: 4123, 4124/ Sunan Ibn Maajah: 3964/ & Musnad Ahmad: 19093/-from the hadeeth of Abu Moosa al-'Ashar'ee. It was Declared authentic by Sheikh al-Albaanee in Saheeh Sunan Abu Dawud and in Saheeh Sunan an-Nasaa'ee.

7- To avoid having an inclination or partiality towards those who are unjust, due to the statement of the Most High, *And incline not toward those who do wrong, lest the Fire should touch you...*-( Surah Hud:113) as well as the statement of the Most High, *And had We not made you stand firm, you would nearly have inclined to them a little. In that case, We would have made you taste a double portion (of punishment) in this life and a double portion (of punishment) after death. And then you would have found none to help you against Us.*-(Surah al-Isra'a:74-75). And Imaam Ahmad narrates in his collection of hadeeth, his 'Musnad', on the authority of Jaabir, may Allaah be pleased with him, that the Messenger of Allaah, may Allaah's praise and His salutations be upon him and his household, said, *{Oh Ka'b Ibn 'Ujrah! Seek refuge in Allaah from the disgraceful rulers.' He said, "Who are the disgraceful rulers, oh Messenger of Allaah?' He said, "Those rulers who will come after me but will not adhere to my Sunnah and not be guided by my guidance. As for those who affirm their lies and deceptions and assist them upon the injustice they commit, then these people are not from me and I am not from them, and they will not approach the cistern on the Day of Judgment. Those who do not affirm their lies and do not assist them upon the injustices they commit, then these people are from me and I am from them, and they will come to the cistern on the Day of Judgment.}* [6]. And I have mentioned this Hadeeth with its chain of narration in the second edition of the book *((as-Saheeh al-Musnad min ad-Dalaa'il an-Nabuwwah)06-44),* and its complete discussion can be found there.

---

[6]    Narrated in Musnad Ahmad: 14860/ -from the hadeeth of Jaabir Ibn 'Abdullah, which was Declared authentic by Sheikh al-Albaanee in Saheeh at-Targheeb wa al-Tarheeb: 2242; & Musnad Ahmad: 17660 -from the hadeeth of Ka'ab Ibn Ujrah, and Sheikh Muqbil stated was acceptable level of authenticity in Saheeh al-Musnad min Dala'il an-Nabuwwah page 562. Likewise Sheikh al-Albaanee stated in Dhelaal al-Jannah: 759 regarding the hadeeth of Hudhaifah– *'It's chain of narration is good'*.

8- To emigrate from that land in which it is not possible for the Muslim to establish his religion, or one in which he fears he will be placed in a prison of the unjust rulers -who are truly "terrorists"- and may be possibly be tortured beyond what he could bear.

9- To make supplications that Allaah shake the feet of the unjust rulers and that He place the best of those from amongst the Muslims in authority over them.

10- To stay away from the causes of separation and differing. From the greatest causes of separation is the arrogance of some of the groups over others and their spreading of wicked statements among people. Allaah the Most Perfect and the Most High says, *And say to My slaves that they should (only) say those words that are the best. (Because) Shaytaan verily, sows disagreements among them. Surely, Shaytaan is to humanity a plain enemy.* -(Surah al-Isra':53). And He said, *The good deed and the evil deed cannot be equal. Repel (the evil) with one which is better (i.e. Allaah ordered the faithful believers to be patient at the time of anger, and to excuse those who treat them badly), then verily! he, between whom and you there was enmity, (will become) as though he was a close friend.*-(Surah Fusilat:34). Also from the causes of division is arguing and disputing based upon falsehood, as is seen in that which Imaam at-Tirmidhee narrated in his well known hadeeth collection on the authority of Abee Umaamah, may Allaah be pleased with him, where he said, The Messenger of Allaah said, *{A people have not gone astray after being guided except that they entered into the practice of disputing.' Then he recited the verse, *They quoted not the above example except for argument. Nay! But they are a quarrelsome people.'*-(Surah Zukhruf: 58).}* [7]. Imaam at-Tirmidhee stated that this hadeeth was authentic.

[7]    Narrated in Jaame' at-Tirmidhee: 3253/ Sunan Ibn Maajah: 48/ & Musnad Ahmad: 21660, 21701/ -from the hadeeth of Abu Imaamah Sadee Ibn 'Ajlaan, which was declared it of a acceptable level of authenticity by Sheikh al-Albaanee in Saheeh at-Targheeb wa al-Tarheeb: 141, and he stated that it was authentic in his checking of Mishkaat al-Masaabeeh: 180, and Sheikh Muqbil declared it authentic in al-Jaame' as-Saheeh: 116, 3783, 4288, 4523.

11- To free yourself from the following of desires. Allaah, the Most Perfect and the Most High says, *But if they answer you not, then know that they only follow their own desires. And who is more astray than one who follows his own desires, without guidance from Allaah? Verily! Allaah guides not the people who are wrong-doers.* -(Surah al-Qasas: 50).

12- To seek beneficial knowledge, and to travel to the scholars of the Sunnah, and to understand the source texts as the first generations understood them. Proceed upon this endeavor by benefiting from two tremendous books, the first of which is the book, *((Jaame'a Bayaan al-'Ilm wa Fadhlihee)12-01)* of Hafidh Ibn Abdul-Bar, and the second book is *((ar-Rihlah)12-08)* by al-Hafidh al-Khateeb. Then your understanding will be built upon what you have read from the understanding of the first generations of Muslims. This is in order that you stand in a position of safety from slipping, as the people involved in ways of innovation usually slip into error, or from the weakening and compromising in your affairs, as many of the modern callers have weakened and compromised theirs. I ask Allaah for guidance for them and us, ameen.

13- To separate yourself from falsehood and its people, with the exception of interacting with them for the purpose of calling them to Allaah. Indeed the believer who mixes with the people and is patient with what he suffers from them is better than the one who does not mix with them and so is not patient with what he will suffer from them, as is affirmed on the Prophet, may Allaah's praise and His salutations be upon him and his household.

14- That you love for the sake of Allaah and hate for the sake of Allaah. Allaah, the Most Perfect and the Most High says, ❦*Oh you who believe! Whoever from among you turns back from his religion (Islaam), Allaah will bring a people whom He will love and they will love Him; humble towards the believers, stern towards the disbelievers...*❧-(Surah al-Maidah:54). And the evidences related to loving for the sake of Allaah and hating for the sake of Allaah are numerous. Our brother Muhammad Ibn Saeed Ibn Salim al-Qahtanee has encompassed most of them in his worthy book, *((al-Walaa' wa al-Baraa' Fee al-Islaam Min Mafaahem Aqeedatul as-Salaf)12-38)*. I advise the reading of this book and benefiting from it.

15- I warn them against those who are actually scholars of evil, so that such individuals are not able to disguise and conceal from you the true nature of their behavior and conduct, as Allaah, the Most Perfect and the Most High said, ❦*Oh you who believe! Verily, there are many of the (Jewish) rabbis and the (Christian) monks who devour the wealth of mankind in falsehood, and hinder (them) from the Way of Allaah*❧-(Surah at-Tawbah:34).

16- Be warned against the regulating and the influencing of the endeavors to call to Allaah by the rulers and those scholars who receive salaries; as the rulers actually seek to diffuse and dissolve the various calls related to Islaam, fearing for their own power and authority. Yet those acquainted with those who truly call to Allaah know that they are not interested in taking positions of authority but only give importance to rectifying the people of the Muslim Ummah as well as their leaders.

17- I advise them to revisit and reconsider the issues or conflicts that stand between each other and review their statements and writings regarding each other, and to consider carefully their behavior in regard to the problems that they face among themselves. The enemies of Islaam may seek to promote a specific individual from the ranks of the people of the Sunnah or the one who is affiliated with them, if they do not heal and reconcile the wounds or problems that exists between them.

18- To warn against the people of falsehood according to the limits of your ability and expose their falsehoods, whether this is within the various forms of media or through writing about it. And we consider both of these acts from us a defensive effort and from those which defend Islaam.

So these are quickly offered brief points of advice to the youth of the Islamic revival. I had previously written it in the fourth issue of the magazine [[al-Bayaan]], and it was entitled, *((My Advice to the People of the Sunnah)12-13)*. Additionally, I had written it and supplemented it in an article entitled, *((This Is Our Call and Our Belief)12-17)*. And all praise is due to Allaah both of these are printed. I also sent it to the magazine 'al-Istiqaamah' as *((My Advice to the People of Hadeeth)12-39)*. I hope that you will read these three advices, as each of them complements the others. I also have written in the last section of *((The Sharp Sword against the Apostasy of the Disbelieving Communists)11-02)*, my recommendations to the Muslim rulers. And the books *((The Exit from the Tribulation)11-21)* and *((The Sharp Sword... )11-02)* both encompass my various advices for the students of knowledge. And Allaah is the one who grants success. We trust in Allaah that these efforts put forward for His sake, He will not allow them to be squandered nor wasted.

*[FROM 'THE STRUGGLE': PAGES 100- 106]*

# (2)

QUESTION: WHAT IS THE CORRECT AND SOUND POSITION TO BE ADOPTED BY THE SCHOLAR, THE STUDENT OF KNOWLEDGE, AND THE CALLER TO ALLAAH IN RELATION TO THE MODERN DAY GROUPS, PARTIES, AND ISLAMIC ORGANIZATIONS?

nswer: The position of the scholar, the caller to Allaah, and the student of knowledge- indeed the position of every Muslim- is that it is obligatory upon him to remind these groups to remember Allaah, the Most Perfect and the Most High, and to warn them about the consequences of separation and differing. They must also warn them about the deviations which have occurred among the youth due to these various groups and parties. Indeed from the present complaints is that there is such and such group, which is established and calls to itself. Then there is this other party which is established and calls to itself, and another which is established, and also calls to itself. So this leaves a young person confused, not knowing whom he should follow- and more than one of our brothers has complained to us of this. Therefore, it is necessary for the students of knowledge and the callers to Allaah to make clear their freedom and disassociation from these various parties and groups.

All praise is due to Allaah, we have an audio cassette which is entitled '*My Advice to the Scholars & Disassociation from Partisanship*'. In addition, from the blessings of Allaah related to this audio lecture is that it was heard by some of the righteous scholars of Najd in Saudi Arabia; and they declared themselves free from group division and partisanship and turned themselves away from it. And perhaps what may have occurred is that they had forgotten or had become accustomed to the prevailing conditions, as otherwise its evidences certainly would have the effect of causing them to act upon them previously.

It has now become apparent that the people of partisanship and separation are ashamed that one of them might openly say, [I am a person upon partisanship to this group.] And at times some of them actually swear and go to the length of saying, [By Allaah! I am not a person of group partisanship!] But he is one who travels from Sana'a to Ma'rib for the purpose of calling to his group, and then from Sana'a to Aden calling to his group, and from Sana'a to Hadhramaut- still calling to his group. And I do not know the extent of how much deception and trickery has occurred here in Yemen through this statement, [By Allaah! I am not a person of group partisanship!] Or perhaps he does not understand the true meaning of partisanship. In actuality, the people are only divided into two groups: into the party of ar-Rahman, The Merciful, and into the party of Shaytaan.

And all praise is due to Allaah that the significant and respected scholars have come to truly understand the seriousness of the partisanship. So that it is said: 'Those scholars who ceased following the correct methodology which we invite you towards- even their students have left them, such that you will see that he is now alone with no one left to teach!'

This is a clear trend among them. In any case, all praise is due to Allaah, many of the youth now perceive and understand the danger of partisanship.

As for the issue of disassociation from it and those upon it, then this is a required matter, as they are considered people upon innovation in the religion. The Messenger of Allaah, may Allaah's praise and His salutations be upon him and his household, said, *{...every innovation is a going astray.}* [1].

And he said, *{Allaah is separated from the repentance of every person of innovation in the religion until he abandons his innovation.}* [2].

---

[1]    Narrated in Saheeh Muslim: 876/ Sunan an-Nasaa'ee: 1579/ Sunan Ibn Maajah: 45/ Musnad Ahmad: 13924/ & Sunan ad-Daaramee: 206- from the hadeeth of Jaabir Ibn 'Abdullah. And it is in Sunan Abu Daawud: 4607/ Sunan Ibn Maajah: 42/ Musnad Ahmad: 16694, 16695/ & Sunan ad-Daaramee: 90/-from the hadeeth of al-'Irbaadh Ibn Saareeyah. Declared authentic by Sheikh al-Albaanee in Silsilatul-Hadeeth Saheehah: 2735, and in Saheeh at-Targheeb at-Tarheeb: 37.

[2]    Narrated in Sunan Ibn Maajah: 50/- from the hadeeth of 'Abdullah Ibn 'Abbaas, by Sheikh al-Albaanee judged it to be an unacceptable narration in Silsilatul-Hadeeth adh-Dha'eefah: 1492, but authenticated a different but similar narration from 'Anas Ibn Maalik *"Indeed Allaah is shielded or separated from the repentance of every individual upon innovation in the religion until he abandons his innovation"* in Saheeh at-Targheeb at-Tarheeb: 37.

So the nature or level of the deviation of innovating in the religion is that it stands on the verge of reaching the level of disbelief in the religion itself. Therefore, if one has allegiance solely for the sake of a group or party or has enmity and disassociation solely for the sake of a group or party, then we fear that he may eventually fall into greater disbelief. As Allaah says, ❖ *Verily, your Wali (Protector or Helper) is Allaah, His Messenger, and the believers; those who perform as-Salaat, and give zakaat, and they bow down.* ❖-(Surah Maidah: 55)

Indeed after all this that has preceded and been made clear, I do not truly know where the intellects of many of the today's youth are! The people of partisanship and separation have been repeatedly exposed and uncovered time and time again, but we still see that some of the youth follow after and remain with them. And this can only be for some worldly benefit, not truly for the sake of the religion. And from Allaah alone we seek assistance from this unfortunate state.

[FROM 'BRIDLING THE RESISTANT ONE': PAGE 385 ]

# (3)

REGARDING KNOWLEDGE:
ITS MERITS, AND WHICH
KNOWLEDGE IS CONSIDERED
OBLIGATORY

ll praise is due to Allaah, Lord of all the worlds, may Allaah's praise and His salutations be upon our prophet Muhammad, the Truthful, and upon his family and all of his Companions. And I bear witness that there is none worthy of worship except Allaah alone Who has no partner. And I bear witness that Muhammad is His worshiper and Messenger. To proceed: The subject which has been selected is the subject of knowledge. Knowledge is considered the cure for all of our illnesses and afflictions. Our prophet Muhammad, may Allaah's praise and salutations be upon him and his household, was ordered by his Lord to ask for an increase in knowledge.

Allaah, the Most Perfect and the Most High, said, ❀*Say: "My Lord! Increase me in knowledge.*❀-(Surah Ta-Ha: 114). And the Lord of Might has explained the condition of the scholar and the condition of the one who is ignorant when He says, ❀*Shall he then who knows that what has been revealed unto you from your Lord is the truth be like him who is blind? But it is only the men of understanding that pay heed.*❀-(Surah ar-Ra'd:19).

And our prophet Muhammad, may Allaah's praise and salutations be upon him and his household, said, in what is narrated in the hadeeth of Mu'aweeyah, may Allaah be pleased with him, transmitted by both Imaams Bukharee and Muslim in their two authentic collections of hadeeth: *{Whoever Allaah intends good for He grants him understanding in the religion.}* [1].

---

[1]   This hadeeth is found in Saheeh al-Bukhaaree: 71, 3116, 7312/ Saheeh Muslim: 1037/ Sunan Ibn Maajah: 221/ al-Muwatta Maalik: 1300, 1667/ Musnad Imaam Ahmad: 16395: 16404, and other narrations/ Musannaf Ibn Abee Shaybah: 31792/ & Sunan ad-Daaramee: 224, 226/- on the authority of Mu'aweeyah. And it is found in Jaame' al-Tirmidhee: 2645/ Musnad Imaam Ahmad: 2786/ & Sunan ad-Daaramee: 270, 2706/- on the authority of Ibn 'Abbaas. And  it is found in Sunan Ibn Maajah:220/ & Musannaf 'Abdul-Razzaaq: 30851/- on the authority of Abu Hurairah. It was declared authentic by Sheikh al-Albaanee in Saheeh al-Aadab al-Mufrad: 517, Silsilat al-Hadeeth as-Saheehah:1194, 1195, 1196, Saheeh at-Targheeb at-Tarheeb: 67, as well as in other of his books. Sheikh Muqbil declared it authentic in al-Jaame' al-Saheeh: 9, 3123, 4650, may Allaah have mercy upon them both.

And the Lord of Might motivates many in His creation, and He says in a verse from His book, ❖*Verily, in that are indeed signs for men of sound knowledge.*❖-(Surah ar-Rum: 22) and the Exalted says, ❖*And these similitudes We put forward for mankind, but none will understand them except those who have knowledge (of Allaah and His Signs, etc.).'*❖-(Surah Ankabut: 43). The Lord of Might gives preference to the dog with training over the dog that does not have training, making permissible the hunted game caught by the trained dog when the name of Allaah is mentioned, as it is sent to hunt. Then the Most Perfect and the Most High says, ❖*They ask you (Oh Muhammad) what is lawful for them (as food). Say: "Lawful unto you are all kind of good foods which Allaah has made lawful. And those beasts and birds of prey which you have trained as hounds, training and teaching them to catch in the manner as directed to you by Allaah*❖-(Surah al-Ma'idah: 4)

Indeed, Allaah, the Most Perfect and the Most High, informed us that when the hoopoe bird presented his excuse to Sulayman he said, ❖*I have grasped (the knowledge of a thing) which you have not grasped and I have come to you from Saba' (Sheba) with true news.*❖-(Surah al-Naml: 22)

Our Prophet Muhammad, may Allaah's praise and salutations be upon him and his household, encouraged his Ummah towards knowledge, and encouraged the Muslim Ummah towards the best type of knowledge, which is the memorization of the Book. The people of philosophical argumentation and false rhetoric say, [Certainly, the best branch of knowledge is the science of philosophical argumentation, as it discusses Allaah and His characteristics.] This is due to their ignorance of the Book of Allaah and the Sunnah of his Messenger, may Allaah's praise and His salutations be upon him and his household.

Imaam Shaafa'ee, may Allaah have mercy upon him, said, "My ruling on the people of philosophical argumentation and false rhetoric is that they should be confined in prison cells and struck with whips,' and he said, "This is the penalty for the one who takes a substitute for the Book of Allaah, or for the one who turns away from the Book of Allaah.' It is clear that the best type of knowledge is the learning of the Book of Allaah and Sunnah of the Messenger of Allaah, may Allaah's praise and His salutations be upon him and his household. Allaah says, *Allaah will exalt in degree those of you who believe, and those who have been granted knowledge.*-(Surah al-Mujadiah: 11) and, *It is only those who have knowledge among His slaves that fear Allaah.*-(Surah al-Fatir: 28).

The best knowledge is the memorization of the Noble Qur'aan, as our Prophet Muhammad, may Allaah's praise and His salutations be upon him and his household, said in the narration of Uthman, may Allaah be pleased with him, found in Saheeh al-Bukhaaree: *{The best of you are those who learn the Qur'aan and teach it.}* [2].

He also said, as found in Saheeh Muslim in the narration of 'Umar, may Allaah be pleased with him, *{Certainly Allaah elevates by this Book some people and lowers and disgraces others by it.}* [3].

From our scholars in the first centuries, may Allaah have mercy upon them, there were those who specialized in the study of the Qur'aan, and those who specialized in the study of the Sunnah of the Messenger of Allaah, may Allaah's praise and His salutations be upon him and his household, as well as those who specialized in the Arabic language. And in most cases the one who specialized in one field or area also

[2]  Narrated in Saheeh al-Bukhaaree: 5027/ Sunan Abee Dawud: 1352/Sunan at-Tirmidhee: 2907/ & Musnad Ahmad: 414, 502/ from the hadeeth of 'Uthmaan Ibn 'Afaan. Declared authentic by Sheikh al-Albaanee in Silsilatul-Hadeeth Saheehah: 1173, and in Saheeh at-Targheeb wa at-Tarheeb: 1415, as well as in other of his works.

[3]  Narrated in Saheeh Muslim: 817/ Sunan Ibn Maajah: 218/ Musnad Ahmad: 233/ & Sunan ad-Daaramee: 3360/ -from the hadeeth of 'Umar Ibn al-Khattab. Declared authentic by Sheikh al-Albaanee in Silsilatul-Hadeeth Saheehah: 2239, Saheeh al-Jaame'a as-Sagheer: 1896, as well as in other of his works.

had a basic proficiency of the other branches of knowledge. However, there were also those like Hafs Ibn Sulaymaan, who was a leader in the branch of the science of recitation of the Qur'aan, as he was one of the well known seven scholars in the science of recitation; yet in the area of hadeeth and its narrations he is rejected as a narrator. There would also be one who was a leader in the science of the hadeeth narrations, but who would make grammar mistakes in simple matters, such as Uthmaan Ibn Abee Shaaybah the blood brother of both Qaasim and Abee Bakr Ibn Abee Shaaybah. He was a leading scholar in the sciences of hadeeth but would commit mispronunciations in the recitation of the Qur'aan. Even though Haafidh Ibn Katheer denies this about him in his well-known book on the science of hadeeth, *((Mukhtasir Ulum al-Hadeeth )04-24)*.

From our scholars from the first centuries of this Ummah were those who specialized in the Arabic language; and indeed the knowledge of Arabic has several branches and areas. There were those who specialized in grammar, which is related to the structure of statements; and those who specialized in linguistic morphology, which is related to the various forms of words; as well as in other areas of the language. There were also those who combined proficiency in more than one area of knowledge. An example of this is Imaam Shaafa'ee, may Allaah have mercy upon him, who was a leading scholar in the field of language, such that he presented arguments by means of his expert knowledge of Arabic. However, he was also a leading scholar in the knowledge of the Sunnah of the Messenger of Allaah, may Allaah's praise and salutations be upon him and his household, such that he was given the title, "One who brings victory to the Sunnah". Two of the books he authored, *((Mukhtalif al-Hadeeth )04-25)* and *((ar-Risaalah )08-03)*, both prove that indeed he was worthy of being given the title "One who brings victory to the Sunnah," as he refuted the people of unrestricted opinions, the sect of the Mu'tazilah, as well as those who slandered and defamed the Sunnah of the Messenger of Allaah, may Allaah's praise and salutations be upon him and his household.

So knowledge has a distinguished and prominent position; and due to this there is rarely an author or compiler who does not include in his work a section generally related to knowledge. In the book Saheeh al-Bukhaaree there is the "Book of Knowledge', and in the book Saheeh Muslim there is the 'Book of Knowledge', and in the work al-Jaame'a at-Tirmidhee there is the 'Book of Knowledge'. Additionally, the people of knowledge have authored works individually devoted to the subject of knowledge, such as al-Haafidh Ibn 'Abdul-Bar Yusuf Ibn 'Abdullah, as he compiled a priceless book which is equal to the value of this entire world, entitled, *((Jaame'a Bayaan al-'Ilm wa Fadhlehe)06-44)*. Within this book he mentions the merit of the scholars, the merits of knowledge, and discusses the issue of blind following. And blind following is not from knowledge, as has been stated, "*The scholars have agreed upon the fact that it is not proper to claim that one who blindly follows is from the people of knowledge.*" And the Lord of Might says in His book, ◈ **Follow what has been sent down unto you from your Lord, and follow not any protectors and helpers, besides Him (Allaah). Little do you remember!** ◈-(Surah al-Araaf:3) So, this worthy book begins with a discussion of the obligation of knowledge, and then proceeds to the hadeeth, *{Seeking knowledge is an obligation upon every Muslim.}* [4] and then he, may Allaah have mercy upon him, indicates that he has judged this narration to be weak. However, Imaam as-Suyootee, may Allaah the Exalted have mercy upon him, stated, "This narration has fifty different complementing routes of transmission,' and therefore judges that the narration was authentic.

---

[4]   Narrated in Sunan Ibn Maajah: 224/ -from the hadeeth of 'Anas Ibn Maalik. Declared authentic by Sheikh al-Albaanee in Saheeh al-Jaame'a as-Sagheer: 1173, in Saheeh at-Targheeb wa at-Tarheeb: 72, as well as in other of his works.

### What is the knowledge that is considered obligatory?

The knowledge that Allaah requires you personally to learn is the knowledge that is considered obligatory upon you as an individual. Included in this are the basic beliefs of Islaam, and these are obligatory upon every Muslim to learn, as is indicated in the Book of Allaah and the Sunnah. It is prohibited that one be ignorant of the basic beliefs of Islaam, whether that be related to the names of Allaah or His characteristics. It is obligatory to believe and affirm our creed regarding Allaah's names and attributes, just as they appear in the Book of Allaah, and as they appear in the Sunnah of the Messenger of Allaah, may Allaah's praise and salutations be upon him and his household. Such as stated clearly by the slave girl who was a shepherdess over a flock of sheep as found in the narration of Mu'aweeyah Ibn al-Hakim, may Allaah be pleased with him, when he came with a slave girl in order to free her. He said: *{ "Messenger of Allaah, I wish to grant her freedom.' He (the Messenger of Allaah, may Allaah's praise and salutations be upon him) said to her, "Oh slave girl, where is Allaah?' She said, "He is in the heavens." He said, "Free her as she is a believing woman."}* [5].

So it is obligatory upon every Muslim to believe that Allaah is in the heavens in a manner befitting His Majesty, and that Allaah the Most Perfect and the Most High is with each of us in His complete knowledge, and through His protection, preservation, and granting of victory to the believers. It is obligatory upon us to believe in this fully, as Allaah says, ❖*Do you feel secure that He, Who is over the heaven (Allaah), will not cause the earth to sink with you, then behold it shakes (as in an earthquake)?*❖-(Surah Mulk: 16) and ❖*The Most Beneficent rose over the Mighty Throne in a manner that suits His Majesty.* ❖-(Surah Ta-Ha: 5).

---

[5]    Narrated in Saheeh Muslim: 537/ Sunan Abu Dawud: 930, 3283/ Sunan an-Nasaa'ee: 1219/ & Musnad Ahmad: 28818, 28819, 28820/ -from the hadeeth of Mu'aweeyah Ibn Hakim. And in Sunan Abu Dawud: 3283/ & Musnad Ahmad: 7836, from the hadeeth of Abu Hurairah, Declared authentic by Sheikh al-Albaanee in Dhelaal al-Jannah: 489, and in Mukhtasir al-'Uluu, pg. 75.

There is a valuable book written on the subject that I advise my brothers in Allaah to read. That beneficial book is the work *((al-Uluu Lil Aalee al-Ghafaar)06-44)* by Haafidh adh-Dhahabee, may Allaah have mercy upon him. It was summarized by Sheikh Naasiruddeen al-Albaanee, may Allaah the exalted preserve him. Those among the students of knowledge who have the ability to verify works should try to acquire the original book, and one who does not have that ability should acquire the *((summarized version)06-44)* by Sheikh al-Albaanee. And if you are able to acquire both of them, then this is best, as one of them does not remove the need for the other.

*[FROM 'AN OFFERING OF ANSWERS TO SOME OF THE QUESTIONS IN HADEETH TERMINOLOGY': PAGES 8-12]*

# *(4)*

QUESTION: SHOULD WE BEGIN WITH SEEKING KNOWLEDGE OR WITH CALLING TO ALLAAH?

nswer: I advise you to begin with knowledge; as if you begin with knowledge then your words will become statements which are accepted. After this we can then proceed to call to Allaah upon clear knowledge. Allaah, the Most Perfect, the Most High says, *Say "This is my way; I invite unto Allaah with sure knowledge, I and whosoever follows me*-(Surah Yusuf:108). And Allaah, the Most Perfect, the Most High says, *Let there arise out of you a group of people inviting to all that is good, and forbidding all that is forbidden. And it is they who are the successful.*-(Surah Aal-'Imraan: 104) We see from this that one should call to goodness. But the ignorant one cannot not truly know whether he calls to goodness or not. Therefore study, and then proceed to call to Allaah with gentleness and kindness according to the limits of your ability, as gentleness and kindness are the two matters through which Allaah brings forth benefit. As for harshness, then we do not have in our hands the power or authority to fight and oppose those who reject entering into the religion of Islaam, nor do we have in our hands the power or authority to imprison those who deserve the punishment of imprisonment. So the remaining option is the invitation and calling accompanied by gentleness and kindness. We also advise them to sit with the esteemed scholars of all the Muslim lands. And if you are able, then call the people to benefit through lectures, such that if there is a lecture regarding the prayer then it in itself is considered a blow against the deviant sect of the Mukaramah. Or if there is a lecture regarding fasting then it in itself is also considered a blow against the sect of the Mukaramah. Rather, such a gathering of the people itself should be considered a blow against the sect of the Mukaramah.

But you should not say: This lecture did not bring about true benefits because it did not warn against nor discuss the errors of the Mukaramah. No, this is not a requirement, as the Book and the Sunnah both generally refute the Mukaramah. Thus it is not always necessary that you openly say, "*Sayyed so-and-so is astray and leading others astray*". You simply teach the people the Book of Allaah and the Sunnah of the Messenger of Allaah, may Allaah's praise and salutations be upon him and his family. Then, if you come to have the ability to do so, continue to give them advice by publishing in daily newspapers, magazines, as well as through books and audio cassettes. Be persistent with such publishing, as this disturbs and disrupts them, meaning those such as the Mukaramah.

Moreover, if an individual from the Mukaramah is prepared to debate with us, then certainly we are prepared to debate with him. As they only posses deceit, lies, dishonesty, and striving to conceal of the truth. They do not possess the knowledge of "*Allaah said* " or that of "*The Messenger of Allaah said* ", may Allaah's praise and salutations be upon him and his family. So it may happen that you obtain enough knowledge that it enables you to face one of the Mukaramah. In this case, if he begins to put forth false conclusions and incorrect interpretations, such as the one who says, [The prayer is a phrase meaning one of the "secrets of the sheikhs"]. And he means by this that you do not need to pray; it is sufficient for you to guard the "sheikh's" secret. So if they, meaning their "sheikhs", inform you of it, then this is sufficient to fulfill this. Likewise with the issues of the pillars of zakaat, charity, and fasting; they are considered to be fulfilled by guarding the "sheikh's" secret. Then you should say "Let us refer back to the books of language. Do they state regarding the definition of "prayer" or "prayers" that it is considered to mean memorizing the secret statements of the "sheikhs"?" Additionally, you should refer back to the correct explanation of the meaning of the word "prayer" in the Book of Allaah and the Sunnah of the Messenger of Allaah, may Allaah's praise and salutations be upon him and his family.

Moreover, after this like pecking, they quickly perform the prayer. You might pray two rakaat of prayer, while the individual from the Mukaramah performs twenty rakaat in the same period of time almost pecking toward the ground like a bird! Indeed, they do not have in their prayer any calmness and humility. And Allaah, the Most Perfect, the Most High said, *Successful indeed are the believers; those who offer their Salaat (prayers) with all solemnity and full submissiveness.*-(1-2). So it is sufficient that someone perceives from their performance of prayer that they do not possess such submissiveness and humility; and so they are not the successful ones. Similarly, with the issue of the congregational prayer; they do not fulfill it nor see it as an obligation until as they say the "true" Imaam is present. Such that some of their prominent individuals in the city of Sa'ada presently do not pray the Jumu'ah congregational prayer, waiting until the "true" Imaam is present. Yet Allaah, the Exalted and the Most Sublime says in his Noble Book, *Oh you who believe! When the call is proclaimed for the Jumu'ah prayer on the day of Friday, come to the remembrance of Allaah*-(Surah Jumu'ah:9). This verse is general in meaning and not linked to the presence of the Imaam. However right now we don't intend to list every matter that they are upon of evil and disbelief, as we have discussed this in two specific audio cassettes. Rather, I advise my brothers in Islaam to seek knowledge, and by this I do not mean seeking knowledge from attending elementary school, and then secondary school, and then high school, and then a college or university, and after this seeking a master's degree and then a doctorate degree, I do not mean this. I mean that you should seek beneficial knowledge; meaning from the Book of Allaah and the Sunnah of the Messenger of Allaah, may Allaah's praise and salutations be upon him and his family. And perhaps after a period of three years, your level of knowledge may be superior to many of the holders of doctorate degrees. And from Allaah Alone we seek help and assistance.

*[FROM 'A DEFENDING MISSION FROM AUDIO LECTURES UPON THE PEOPLE OF IGNORANCE AND SOPHISTRY': VOL. 1, PAGE 321]*

# (5)

QUESTION: WHAT ARE THE GUIDELINES OF SEEKING KNOWLEDGE AND WHAT ARE THE MEANS AND WAYS OF SEEKING IT?

nswer: In regard to the principles of seeking knowledge: beneficial knowledge begins with the Book of Allaah and its memorization. As the Prophet, may Allaah's praise and salutations be upon him and his family, stated, *{The one who is proficient in reciting the Qur'aan is associated with the noble, upright, recording angels, and the one who makes mistakes in it, and finds difficulty in it, receives have a double reward}*[1] narrated by both Imaams Bukhaaree and Muslim on the authority of 'Aishah, may Allaah be pleased with her. And the Prophet, may Allaah's praise and salutations be upon him and his family, said, *{It will be said to the reciter of the Qur'aan: Read and beautify your recitation, and your place and status will be equal to the last verse you recite}* [2] as collected by at-Tirmidhee on the authority of 'Abdullah Ibn 'Amr Ibn al-Aas.

And the Lord of Might said in His Noble Book, ❖*Verily, this Qur'aan guides to that which is most just and right...*❖- (Surah al-Isra':9) And He says, ❖*And We send down of the Qur'aan that which is a cure and a mercy to the believers, and it increases the wrongdoers in nothing but loss.*❖-(Surah al-Isra':82). Therefore it is upon the student to start with the memorization of the Qur'aan. As you have also been commanded, begin along with your memorization of the Qur'aan those additional matters which Allaah has obligated upon you. For example, in the area of correct beliefs you should study a basic summarized book, whether this be *((al-Aqeedatul-Wasateeyah)06-05)* by Sheikh al-Islaam Ibn Taymeeyah or *((Tatheer al-Itiqaad)06-30)* by Imaam San'anee. Both of them are simple, easy works, all praise is

[1] Narrated in Saheeh al-Bukhaaree: 4937/ Saheeh Muslim: 798/ Sunan Abee Dawud: 1454/ Jaame'a al-Tirmidhee: 2904/Sunan Ibn Maajah: 3779 / Musnad of Imaam Ahmad: 23691, 24113, and others- on the authority of 'Aishah Mother of the Believers. It was declared authentic by Sheikh al-Albaanee in Irwaa' al-Ghaleel: 2598, and in Saheeh Sunan Abu Dawud 1454 and Saheeh Sunan at-Tirmidhee 2904.

[2] Narrated in Sunan Abee Dawud: 1454/ Jaame'a al-Tirmidhee: 2904 /-on the authority of 'Abdullah Ibn 'Amr. It was declared authentic by Sheikh al-Albaanee in Silsilat al-Hadeeth As-Saheehah: 2240 Irwaa' al-Ghaleel: 2598, and in Mishkaat al-Masaabeeh: 2134. Sheikh Muqbil declared it authentic in al-Jaame'a al-Saheeh: 54.

due to Allaah. Then proceed to study whatever Allaah has required of you and this is the meaning of the statement of the Prophet, may Allaah's praise and salutations be upon him and his family: *{Seeking knowledge is an obligation upon every Muslim}* [3]. So if you intend to pray you should understand how the Messenger of Allaah, may Allaah's praise and salutations be upon him and his family, prayed, as he said, *{Pray as you see me praying.}* [4]. And if you intend to make obligatory pilgrimage of Hajj, you must first understand how the Messenger of Allaah, may Allaah's praise and salutations be upon him and his family, made pilgrimage, as he said, *{Take from my actions your rites of pilgrimage.}* [5]. Likewise, this is the case with the zakaat charity and other matters. If you are engaged in the affairs of buying and selling then it is necessary that you understand the rulings of the Sharee'ah regarding buying and selling. And the knowledge of the Book and the Sunnah is simple. As the Lord of might says in His Noble Book, *And We have indeed made the Qur'aan easy to understand and remember; then is there anyone who will remember*-(Surah Qamar:17) And the Prophet, may Allaah's praise and salutations be upon him and his family, said, *{I was sent with the straightforward Hanafeeyah.}* [6] meaning the naturally simple worship of Allaah alone . What actually ends up making knowledge complicated are the people. From the best sayings is the one who said,

[3]    Narrated in Sunan Ibn Maajah: 224 /-on the authority of Anas Ibn Maalik. It was declared authentic by Sheikh al-Albaanee in Mishkaat al-Masaabeeh: 218, in Saheeh al-Jaame'a as-Sagheer 3813,3914, in Saheeh at-Targheeb wa at-Tarheeb 72 and in Saheeh Sunan Ibn Maajah.
[4]    Narrated in Saheeh al-Bukhaaree: 613, 5669/ - on the authority of Maalik Ibn Huwayreth. It was declared authentic by Sheikh al-Albaanee in Saheeh al-Aadab al-Mufrad: 216.
[5]    Narrated in Saheeh Muslim: 1297/ Sunan Abu Dawud: 1970/ Sunan an-Nisaa'ee: 3064 / Musnad of Imaam Ahmad: 14208, 14623/- on the authority of Jaabir Ibn 'Abdullah. It was declared authentic by Sheikh al-Albaanee in Hajj an-Nabee: 85, and Saheeh Sunan Abu Dawud.
[6]    Narrated in Musnad of Imaam Ahmad: 21788- on the authority of Abu Imaamah Sadee Ibn Ajlaan. It was declared authentic by Sheikh al-Albaanee in Silsilat al-Hadeeth as-Saheehah: 2924.

*If it was not for the worldly rivalry by offering similar books,*

　　　*there would not be books named 'Mugnee' or 'Amdah',*

*They legitimize them by claiming that they solves complex issues,*

　　　*but in the books which are produces, the problems of complexity simply increased*

And Sharstaanee explained quite clearly his own confusion:

*I wandered around all the different centers of theoretical*

*or speculative study*

　　　*passing my sight between their various different teachers,*

*I did not see except the one who had sadly held his chin in his hand or the frustrated one who gritted his teeth in sorrow and regret.*

Imaam as-Sanaanee came across these two verses of poetry and criticized them, saying:

*I fear that you failed to travel to the center of the true people of the Messenger*

　　　*nor those who have allegiance to him from every true scholar,*

*For the one who guided by the guidance of Muhammad is not confused*

　　　*nor will you see him gritting his teeth in frustration and regret.*

And Raazee said after squandering his years away in philosophy and then later returning back to the guidance of the Book of Allaah and the Sunnah:

*The end result of the building the intellect upon the
unrestricted ideas of the mind is only shackles*

> *and the inevitable conclusion of that worthless
> endeavor is nothing other than a false empty
> accomplishment,*

*Our spirits became hateful within our own bodies,*

> *and the end of our worldly life was only destruction
> and evil consequences*

*We did not benefit at all from this path we took in seeking
truth nor the great length of time spent of our efforts,*

> *Except that we gathered in that period, only the
> worthlessness of this one said that and other one said
> this.*

And Ayyub as-Sakhtiyaanee said, "*From the true success
of an individual is Allaah guiding him to the Sunnah from
the beginning of his youth.*" But consider the example of the
one who passes through a stage of involvement with Sufism,
and then moved on to a period of participation in group
partisanship and various movements, and then slips from
this to involving himself with prohibited entertainments
such as movies and other matters which simply waste time,
and then finally sucessfully moves on to an attachment to
the Sunnah, how much of his time has been wasted and
lost?! The Prophet, may Allaah's praise and salutations be
upon him and his family, said, *{A servant of Allaah will not
move his feet from his place on the Day of Judgment until he
is asked about four matters..}* [7] and from them is his time
and how he spent it. Yet someone who is granted success to
adhere to the Sunnah early on, it is possible that after two or
three years of study, with the permission of Allaah, he may

---

[7]   Narrated in Jaame'a at-Tirmidhee: 2417/ & Sunan ad-Daaramee: 537/ -on the
authority of Abu Burzah al-'Aslamee. It was declared authentic by Sheikh al-Albaanee in
Saheeh al-Jaame'a as-Sagheer: 7300, and he stated in his verification of 'Iqtida'a al-'Ilm al-
'Amal, "It chain of narration is authentic"

become a reviewer, author, a verifier of hadeeth, or whatever Allaah, by virtue of His power, enables him to accomplish. So it is essential that he make his focus upon worldly affairs secondary to seeking knowledge, and does not make seeking knowledge secondary to worldly affairs. Allaah will not allow your efforts to be wasted.

*[FROM 'A DEFENDING MISSION FROM AUDIO LECTURES UPON THE PEOPLE OF IGNORANCE AND SOPHISTRY': VOL. 2, PAGE 373]*

$(6)$

QUESTION: WHAT IS YOUR ADVICE FOR
THE BEGINNER IN SEEKING SHAREE'AH
KNOWLEDGE?

nswer: This is a wide area of discussion, as beginners vary and are on different levels. Among them are those who do not have the ability to write well, therefore it is proper that they begin with learning how to write. But there are those who write well so this will be easy upon them, if Allaah wills. So what remains is that they begin with the fundamentals of knowledge. The Messenger, upon him be the best of greetings and the best mention in the heavens by Allaah and His angels, said when he sent Mu'adh to Yemen, *{Certainly you will be coming to a people from the people of the previously revealed books, so make the first matter that you invite them to be bearing witness that there is none worthy of worship but Allaah alone and that Muhammad is the Messenger of Allaah.}* [1]. It is an issue of proceeding by stages no matter whether that occurs at the beginning of your seeking knowledge or an advanced level. It is not proper that someone study alone a great deal, as this will only leave partial traces of knowledge he has studied. When Imaam Shaafa'ee passed by a teacher of the child of the Muslim ruler he said, *"Do not convey to him the entirety of this branch of knowledge until he has mastered its fundamentals. Because if you transmit this area of knowledge to him as a whole before he has properly mastered it fundamentals, it will leave him with only fragments or portions of the knowledge he has studied."* So this is one matter. An additional matter, as Imaam Shaafa'ee, may Allaah have mercy upon him states, *"Certainly, memorization and understanding are two gifts from Allaah, the Most Perfect, the Most High."*

So the people differ in their level of possessing them. If you see a man who is able to memorize two pages a day from the Qur'aan, and you are not able to do that, then we advise you to memorize a single page. And perhaps your

---

[1] Narrated in Saheeh al-Bukhaaree: 1496, 4347/-on the authority of 'Abdullah Ibn 'Abbaas. And it is found in Saheeh Muslim: 19/-on the authority of Mu'adh Ibn Jabal. It was declared authentic by Sheikh al-Albaanee in Saheeh al-Jaame'a as-Sagheer: 2298 from the hadeeth of Ibn 'Abbaas.

understanding of it will be stronger and firmer than the one who memorizes the two pages. And some of the people may be able to memorize an entire thirtieth of the Qur'aan in single day, as this is simply from the blessings of Allaah, the Most High, the most Exalted. And from Allaah alone we seek assistance and support. However, undertaking too many lessons, and burdening of oneself with what you are not able to bear, will be the cause of your ruin.

*[FROM 'THE FINAL TRAVELS OF THE IMAAM OF THE ARAB PENINSULA', BY UMM SALAMAH AS-SALAFEEYAH, PAGE 233]*

# (7)

QUESTION: FOR THE BEGINNING STUDENT
OF KNOWLEDGE, FOR EXAMPLE IN
AMERICA, WHAT IS YOUR ADVICE REGARDING
THOSE BOOKS WHICH HE SHOULD BEGIN
WITH AND THEN THOSE TO PROCEED TO STEP
BY STEP?

nswer: If he is able to sit with a scholar and have him instruct and guide him upon the path of seeking knowledge, then this is a good way. Indeed, instruction through the scholars and the influence of the relationship that is between the student and his teacher will help make clear and evident within the mind of the student- what knowledge his sheikh relates to him. This method of instruction is a remarkable thing in terms of what is received and what is given back. So if this is easy then we advise him with this initially, and if that is not something possible for him then we advise him to begin with summarized books such as the book, *((A Beneficial Statement Regarding the Evidences of Tawheed)06-19)* by our brother in Islaam Sheikh Muhammad Ibn 'Abdul-Wahaab al-'Abdalee al-Wasaabee, and likewise the book, *((Thalaathatul-Usul)06-02)* by Sheikh Muhammad Ibn 'Abdul-Wahaab an-Najdee, may Allaah have mercy upon him, and also *((al-Aqeedatul-Wasateeyah)06-05)* by Sheikh al-Islaam Ibn Taymeeyah.

The student should dedicate time to the memorization of the Qur'aan. If he has the ability to memorize, then it is proper that he designates a large portion of his time for the memorization of the Qur'aan. This follows that which we mentioned regarding it. If he is a non-Arab, then we advise him to give importance to learning the Arabic language. This is because our brothers from the non-Arabs are quick to accept and follow the one who has strength in the Arabic language. Many people responded to the false call of Khomaynee, and the majority of those who responded were non-Arabs. Additionally many people responded to the false call of the Qaadeeanees, and many people responded to the false call of the Tijaanee Sufees because they had with them upon their way those who were strong in the Arabic language. Therefore, we advise our brothers from the non-Arabs to give importance to learning the Arabic language, such that if you draw a conclusion regarding a matter of the religion, you will understand whether your conclusion is properly derived or not. However, if one of our brothers is not from the non-Arabs then he should begin with the study of correct beliefs. Additionally, it is also important for the non-Arabs to proceed by small steps, in moderate amounts. We have ended with this part of the advice.

After this, if Allaah wills, perhaps a scholar can educate his students by the study of a single hadeeth from *((Saheeh al-Bukhaaree)02-01)* and benefit them with its proper understanding, as well as studying Imaam al-Bukhaaree's biography, as many scholars were amazed when encountering the biography of Imaam al-Bukhaaree. In this way, the students will benefit from it regarding both in the understanding of the hadeeth and in regards to the text of narration itself. And they will benefit in knowing how to search for information related to the narrators of the hadeeth, and how one is able to reach the assessment that a hadeeth is authentic or weak. Perhaps only a short period will pass and they will benefit. Additionally, I advise them to specialize. So the one who has the desire to specialize whether it is, as was mentioned, in the study of hadeeth, or if he has a desire to specialize in grammar; then we advise him to settle himself upon that chosen area of grammar. This will allow him to best utilize his free time. So if one has a desire to specialize in hadeeth and the science of hadeeth terminology, then we advise him to do so, and another wishes to specialize in the explanations of Qur'aan or jurisprudence then we advise that he also do so.

In addition to what is mentioned, specializing has a basis in evidence, as Hudhaifah said, "*The people used to ask the Messenger of Allaah, may Allaah's praise and salutations be upon him, regarding good and I used to ask him about evil as I feared that it would come upon me.*" And the Prophet, may Allaah's praise and salutations be upon him, recognized this, even giving him the nickname, 'Holder of the secrets of the

Messenger of Allaah', may Allaah's praise and salutations be upon him. From this we see that specialization is a beneficial matter. After this, we advise that you do not jump into too many lessons, as you will have entered into them but will not understand their various aspects properly, and your condition will become, as one person said:

And he proceeded upon his plans and spent the fruits of his youth, but in the end was uncertain and unsure, without have attained clear successes or failures. So do not undertake more lessons than you have the ability to tolerate and comprehend. And even worse than this is that one of you begin to attend lessons in the subject of correct beliefs, but then you say: "*By Allaah, so-and-so is teaching grammar, and by Allaah's decree he is benefiting his students*", so then he says, "*I will study with him!*" So then he studies for a short period of time in grammar, but eventually says, "So-and-so is now teaching hadeeth science terminology, and he is an ocean of knowledge in the science of hadeeth terminology, Allaah has decreed that he is excelling in this. So I will study hadeeth science terminology with him." Then, another comes along and informs him that someone is teaching the book of Imaam Shawkaanee related to jurisprudence. So now this same student then says "*I will go and study with him.*" and he goes and studies with him, leaving what he had begun studying a short time before.

This is truly a pity and a failure, and it has occurred to more than one individual, among those who become bored easily from the students of knowledge. So no, it is necessary as is said,

*A man stands with his feet firmly upon the earth,*

   *but the highest of his aspirations are in the stars.*

It is necessary that he makes efforts and struggles and has patience with difficulties and hardships, as knowledge is not achieved except through suffering and difficulty, as occurred to our scholars of the first generations, may Allaah the Most High have mercy upon them. And from Allaah we seek help and assistance.

*[FROM 'THE FINAL TRAVELS OF THE IMAAM OF THE ARAB PENINSULA' BY UMM SALAMAH AS-SALAFEEYAH, PAGE 273]*

# (8)

QUESTION: I AM A TEACHER IN AN ISLAMIC SCHOOL, TEACHING BOYS BETWEEN THE AGES OF SEVEN AND ELEVEN VARIOUS STUDIES RELATED TO ISLAAM. WHAT DO YOU ADVISE ME TO TEACH THEM? ALSO, WHICH ARE THE BEST BOOKS FOR THEM IN THE AREA OF FUNDAMENTAL BELIEFS?

nswer: A book that is suitable for them in the area of correct beliefs is the book *((A Beneficial Statement Regarding the Evidences of Tawheed)06-19)* by our brother the esteemed Sheikh Muhammad Ibn 'Abdul-Wahaab al-Wasaabee, and likewise *((Kitaab al-Tawheed)06-01)*, by Sheikh Muhammad Ibn 'Abdul-Wahaab an-Najdee, may Allaah have mercy upon him, and the book *((al-Aqeedatul-Wasateeyyah)06-05)* by Sheikh al-Islaam Ibn Taymeeyah. Then after this if you are able, have them memorize the hadeeth narrations which are found in both the collections of Imaams Bukhaaree and Muslim. We advise that they undertake this with hadeeth narrations such as *{The best of you are those who learn the Qur'aan and teach it}* [1], and such as, *{Islaam is build upon five, bearing witness that there is none worth of worship except Allaah, and that Muhammad is the Messenger of Allaah, to establish the obligatory prayer, pay the obligatory zakaat charity, the obligatory pilgrimage of Hajj, and the obligatory fast}* [2]. This is how this version of the narration is structured: *{...the obligatory pilgrimage of Hajj, and the obligatory fast}* with the wording regarding to Hajj coming before that of fasting, but it is also narrated with the wording related to fasting coming before Hajj in some narrations. Likewise, also give attention to those hadeeth that are authentic but not found within the two 'Saheeh' collections of Imaam al-Bukhaaree and Muslim, such as the narration, *{The one who swears by his faithfulness is not*

---

[1]    Narrated in Saheeh al-Bukhaaree: 5027/ Sunan Abu Daawud: 1452/ Jaame'a at-Tirmidhee: 2907/ & Musnad Imaam Ahmad: 414, 502, -on the authority of 'Uthmaan Ibn 'Afaan. It was declared authentic by Sheikh al-Albaanee in Silsilat al-Hadeeth as-Saheehah:1173, Saheeh at-Targheeb at-Tarheeb: 1415, Mishkaat al-Masaabeh: 2109, Saheeh al-Jaame'a as-Sagheer: 5630, and in other works such as Saheeh Sunan Abu Dawud & Saheeh Sunan at-Tirmidhee.

[2]    Narrated in Saheeh al-Bukhaaree: 8/ Jaame'a at-Tirmidhee: 2709/ Sunan an-Nasaa'ee: 5004/ & Musnad Imaam Ahmad: 4783, 5639, 5979/ -on the authority of 'Abdullah Ibn 'Umar. And it is narrated in Saheeh Muslim: 16/ -on the authority of 'Umar Ibn 'Khattab. It was declared authentic by Sheikh al-Albaanee in Irwa' al-Ghaleel : 781,901,971, Saheeh at-Targheeb at-Tarheeb: 350, 737, and in his verification of 'al-Emaan' by Ibn Taymeeyah pg. 4.

*from us.}* [3], and similar short hadeeth that will remain in the minds of the students. This is what I advise you with, may Allaah bless you.

Then after this, teach them the Arabic language, as the Arabic language is the language of the Qur'aan. As that which is evil came to many of our brothers from the non-Arabs, some of them accept and follow him such as occurred with Khomaynee the Raafidhee, and some of them accepting and following the Qadeeyannes, and some of them accepting and following the Teejanee Sufees, and some of them accepting and following any astray sect which presents itself to them, simply because they themselves do not understand the Arabic language. So every person who calls them to some way and they consider him to have some knowledge, they follow and accept that which he calls them to.

So we advise them or advise our brothers to teach their sons the Arabic language. It is essential and it is the language of the Qur'aan. Allaah, the Most Perfect, the Most High says, *❖An Arabic Qur'aan❖*-(Surah Yusuf:2) and He says, *❖All praise is due to Allaah, Who has sent down to His servant the Book, and has not placed therein any crookedness❖*-(Surah al-Kahf:1) The Qur'aan is in the Arabic language, and the Sunnah of the Messenger of Allaah, may Allaah's praise and salutations be upon him, is in the Arabic language, as are the books of jurisprudence. Therefore it is necessary and essential, to teach their sons the Arabic language until they reach a level of understanding where they become safe and protected from someone inviting them to falsehood that they might respond to due to not knowing Arabic. They may even accept the doubts and false ideas presented

[3] Narrated in Sunan Abu Daawud: 3253/ & Musnad Imaam Ahmad: 22471/ -on the authority of 'Buraydah Ibn al-Haseeb. It was declared authentic by Sheikh al-Albaanee in Silsilat al-Hadeeth as-Saheehah:94, 325, Mishkaat al-Masaabeh: 3420, Saheeh at-Targheeb at-Tarheeb: 2013, 2954, Saheeh al-Jaame'a as-Sagheer: 5436, 6203, as well as in Saheeh Sunan Abu Dawud. Sheikh Muqbil declared it authentic in al-Jaame'a al-Saheeh: 387, 3070, 3280, 4509.

to them by Christian missionaries or others. Perhaps they may approach them with doubts related to alleged errors within the Qur'aan. But the Qur'aan has been supported and given tremendous attention by our scholars, may Allaah the Exalted have mercy upon them for every service they have put forth. They have discussed these apparent issues, all praise is due to Allaah, in the books that are explanations of the Qur'aan as well as in the book *((al-Mughnee)07-07)* of Ibn Qudaamah and other works. So the Arabic language is very important; then after this comes the study of the correct beliefs, and then after this the memorization of what they are able to from the Qur'aan. Next, proceed to the study of what is required to fulfill their need to understand how the Messenger of Allaah, may Allaah's praise and salutations be upon him, prayed, as well as his other deeds and activities. These issues should be given priority over other matters. And from Allaah we seek help and assistance.

*[FROM 'THE FINAL TRAVELS OF THE IMAAM OF THE ARAB PENINSULA' BY UMM SALAMAH AS-SALAFEEYAH PAGE 254]*

# (9)

QUESTION: WHAT ARE THOSE MATTERS WITHIN THE METHODOLOGY OF THE PEOPLE OF THE SUNNAH AND THE JAMA'AH WHICH IT IS PERMISSIBLE TO DIFFER IN, WHILE GIVING ADVICE TO EACH OTHER REMAINS BETWEEN US; AND WHICH MATTERS IS IT IS NOT PERMISSIBLE FOR US TO DIFFER IN? IS IT PERMISSIBLE TO DIFFER IN REGARDS TO THE BASIC CORRECT BELIEF, OR WITH THE DIFFERENT ISSUES OF BELIEF? IN WHAT SOURCE WORK CAN WE FIND A SIMPLE CLARIFICATION OF THIS?

nswer: Differences are divided into several types: the differences of diversity, such as the differing versions of the statements of 'at-tashshahud' in the prayer, and the different forms of sending praise and salutations upon the Prophet, may Allaah's praise and salutations be upon him and his family, and the difference of raising the hands in prayer to the shoulders or to the edges of the two ears. There are many examples of this type. Sheikh al-Islaam Ibn Taymeeyah stated, "*No one disapproves of or censures someone due to differences of diversity except for the ignorant one.*" Then there are differences of understanding; such as that regarding menstruation- is it pure or impure, as linguistically it can have both meanings. In many issues some scholars hold one understanding and other scholars have a different understanding, and this is from the well-grounded esteemed major scholars. This is considered like the differences of understanding which occurred between the Companions, may Allaah be pleased with them all, at the time when the Prophet, may Allaah's praise and salutations be upon him and his family said to them, *{The one who believes in Allaah and the Last Day should not pray Salatul-Asr except in Banee Qurathah.}*[1].Some of the Companions said that what was meant was to begin the journey and then to pray on the way. Others, however, differed and delayed praying until they had actually arrived at Banee Qurathah. So this is a difference of understanding. So it is seen that in issues in which there are differences of diversity or differences of understanding there should be no blaming or censuring the other. When someone blames another in an issue related to differences of understanding, certainly he is calling to blind following him.

The third type of differences is the difference of opposition to the truth. This is when someone opposes the authentic, clear, evidence without any authority or proof. You say to <u>him</u>, "*It is forbidden for a man to wear gold jewelry*", and he

[1]   Narrated in Saheeh al-Bukhaaree: 946, 4119/ Saheeh Muslim: 1770/ -on the authority of 'Abdullah Ibn 'Umar.

says, [This is simply for my engagement celebration.] Or you say to him, "*Elections are giving to another the authority that is Allaah's alone, as part of it is the negotiating of which aspects of the guidance of Islaam should be accepted and practiced.*" So he replies, [We are compelled and forced to this.] But the reality is that they are not compelled to it, rather that they have expanded the Sharee'ah allowance of necessity such that in reality they end up abandoning its guidelines. Therefore opposition to the authentic clear evidence without an explanation is that which is considered a difference of opposition the Sharee'ah. It is this differing that it is necessary that we blame and censure the one who falls into it.

Additionally, differing in the issues of the correct belief is not permissible, as it is a clear, defined matter and the one who differs in this and produces newly invented principles and beliefs is considered an innovator in the religion. If it is said to him, ❧*The Most Gracious rose over the Throne (in a manner befitting His Majesty and Transcendence)*❧-(Surah Ta-Ha: 5) and he replies,[He is everywhere, in everyplace], then he has a serious error in his understanding and is considered an innovator in the religion. As was stated clearly by some of the preeminent people whom Allaah guided their hand such as Sheikh al-Islaam Ibn Taymeeyah. It was said to Sheikh al-Islaam Ibn Taymeeyah, who was given the title of the 'Nobleman' of his age, "*What do you say about those predecessors of yours from the Asharee sect?*" He replied: "*I say that they were in error, and it is improper that we follow them in their errors.*" Additionally, the people of the Sunnah themselves have differed in some matters, such as the issue of Allaah's descending; does Allaah descend in His essence or by His throne? However, this is considered from the secondary matters, as we believe that Allaah descends to the heaven of this world in the last third of the night, but we do not say it occurs in this way nor say it occurs in that way.

As for the hadeeth: *{Allaah created Aadam upon his image.}* [2]. This is found in Saheeh al-Bukhaaree. It is also found outside Saheeh al-Bukhaaree with the wording *{... upon the image of the Merciful}* [3]. However this is version of the narration is weak. Ibn Qutabah said, "*The people of guidance do not censure the connection of an image to Allaah as they did not originate this statement. The Prophet, may Allaah's praise and salutations be upon him and his family, informed us that in what occurs during the time of resurrection Allaah will come upon his own "image"*. So it is correct to affirm an image to Allaah, the Most Glorified and the Most Exalted - in a way which benefits His Majesty and Transcendence.

*[FROM 'A DEFENDING MISSION FROM AUDIO LECTURES UPON THE PEOPLE OF IGNORANCE AND SOPHISTRY': VOL.2, PAGE 51]*

---

[2]     Narrated in Saheeh Muslim: 2612/ & Musnad Imaam Ahmad: 7279, 7372, 9646/ -on the authority of Abu Hurairah. It was declared authentic by Sheikh al-Albaanee in Silsilat al-Hadeeth as-Saheehah:862, Mishkaat al-Masaabeh: 3525, and Dhelaal al-Jannah: 519, 520.

[3]     Narrated in Mu'jam al-Kabeer: 13404/ & as-Sunnah of Ibn Abee 'Asim: 529/ & ash-Sharee'ah of al-'Aajooree: 725/ -on the authority of 'Abdullah Ibn 'Umar. It was declared authentic by Sheikh al-Albaanee in Silsilat al-Hadeeth as-Saheehah: 529, Dhelaal al-Jannah: 517.

# (10)

QUESTION: SOME OF THE PEOPLE OF KNOWLEDGE SAY, "WE ADVISE THE BEGINNING STUDENT TO READ IN THE SUBJECT OF CORRECT BELIEFS, THE BOOK 'AL-AQEEDATUL-WASATEEYAH' AND IN RELATION TO FIQH, OR THE GENERAL UNDERSTANDING OF HOW TO PRACTICE THE RELIGION, TO STUDY THE WORKS OF THE SCHOOL OF JURISPRUDENCE PREDOMINANTLY FOUND WITHIN HIS COUNTRY. THEREFORE IF THE PEOPLE OF THE COUNTRY FOLLOW THE HANBALEE SCHOOL OF JURISPRUDENCE, THEN STUDY FROM THE BOOK 'ZAAD AL-MUSTAQNAA', AND IF THEY FOLLOW THE SHAAFA'EE SCHOOL OF JURISPRUDENCE OR THE MAALIKEE SCHOOL OF JURISPRUDENCE, THEN STUDY FROM THEIR RELEVANT BOOKS." SO WHAT IS THE PROPER WAY TO STUDY THE BRANCH OF KNOWLEDGE KNOWN AS FIQH, AND WHICH BOOKS DO YOU RECOMMEND FOR ITS STUDY? ALSO, WHICH SCHOLAR'S STATEMENTS ARE PRIMARILY BASED UPON THE BOOK AND THE SUNNAH IN THIS FIELD?

nswer: All praise is due to Allaah, Lord of all the worlds, and praise and salutation be upon our Prophet Muhammad, and his family, and all his Companions. I bear witness that there is none worthy of worship except Allaah alone having no partner or associate, and I bear witness that Muhammad is His worshiper and His Messenger. As for what follows: The advice to read the book *((al-Aqeedatul-Wasateeyah)06-05)* is advice that is accepted, as it primarily contains verses of the Qur'aan and hadeeth narrations from the Prophet, may Allaah's praise and salutations be upon him. That work, as well as the book *((Beneficial Statements Regarding the Evidence of Allaah's Right Alone to be Worshiped)06-19)*, of Sheikh Muhammad Ibn 'Abdul-Wahaab al-'Abdalee are considered from the best books in relation to the study of correct beliefs. The book *((al-Aqeedatul-Wasateeyah)06-05)* contains an explanation of Allaah's right to be worshiped alone, as well as the correct principles and understanding of his names and attributes, so it is an invaluable book, may Allaah reward Sheikh al-Islaam Ibn Taymeeyah tremendously for authoring it. As for referring to *((Zaad al-Mustaqna')07-01)*, then I hold that one should refer to the Book of Allaah and the Sunnah of the Messenger of Allaah, may Allaah's praise and salutations be upon him. Our Prophet said during his farewell pilgrimage, as found in the hadeeth of Jaabir narrated in Saheeh Muslim, *{Certainly, I am leaving with you two things which if you hold fast to them, you will not go astray; the Book of Allaah..}* [1] and in the narration of Zayd Ibn Arqam, *{I am leaving you with two weighty things. The first of them is the Book of Allaah, as it contains guidance and light, so take the Book of Allaah and hold fast to it...}* [2].

[1]   Narrated in Saheeh Muslim: 1218/ Jaame'a at-Tirmidhee: 3786/ -on the authority of Jaabir Ibn 'Abdullah.
And it is found in Jaame'a at-Tirmidhee: 3788/ -on the authority of Zayd Ibn 'Arqam. It was declared authentic by Sheikh al-Albaanee in Saheeh al-Jaame'a as-Sagheer: 2458, and in Saheeh Sunan at-Tirmidhee.
[2]   Narrated in Saheeh Muslim: 2408/ Musnad Imaam Ahmad: 18780/

So The Messenger of Allaah, may Allaah's praise and salutations be upon him, encouraged the people to and made them wish to take firm hold of the Book of Allaah.

Then he said: *{And the people of my family, be mindful of your Lord in relation to my family, be mindful of your Lord in relation to my family, be mindful of your Lord in relation to my family.}* Also the Lord of Might and Glory says in His Noble Book, *Follow what has been sent down unto you from your Lord, and follow not any protectors, besides Him (Allaah). Little do you remember!*-(Surah al-Aaraf:3) He also says, *And follow not that of which you have no knowledge. Verily, the hearing, and the sight, and the heart of each of those ones will be questioned by Allaah*-(Surah al-Israa: 36). And He also says, *And whatsoever the Messenger gives you, take it; and whatsoever he forbids you, abstain from it*-(Surah al-Hashr:7) Our Prophet, may Allaah's praise and salutations be upon him, said, *{..Avoid that which I forbid you to do and do that which I command you to do to the best of your capacity. As the people before you were ruined because they had put too many questions to their Prophets and then disagreed with their Prophets' teachings}.* And in the same hadeeth, *{Completely avoid that which I forbid you from doing and do that which I command you to do to the best of your capacity.}* [3]. Therefore our religion in based upon the verses of the Qur'aan and the Prophetic Narrations.

As you may come across expressions and sayings related to issues of menstruation and issues of divorce in the book *((Zaad al-Mustaqna')07-01)* that will preoccupy you and take your time, which are not based upon evidence from the Book of Allaah or the Sunnah; they are considered to be statements of supposition or speculation. So leave of

---

& Sunan ad-Daaramee: 3316/ -on the authority of Zayd Ibn 'Arqam. It was declared authentic by Sheikh al-Albaanee in Saheeh al-Jaame'a as-Sagheer: 1351.
[3] Narrated in Saheeh Muslim: 1337/ Sunan an-Nasaa'ee: 2620/ Sunan Ibn Maajah: 2/ Musnad Imaam Ahmad: 7320, 9890, and other narrations/ -on the authority of Abu Hurairah. It was declared authentic by Sheikh al-Albaanee in Saheeh al-Jaame'a as-Sagheer: 5810.

wrongly thinking that referring to the Qur'aan and Sunnah will require from you a lengthy effort. Indeed, perhaps you may memorize the Qur'aan in a single year and afterwards memorize what you are able to from the Sunnah of the Messenger of Allaah, may Allaah's praise and salutations be upon him, as well as learning the ability to distinguish between what is authentic from what is rejected, and that which has hidden defects from that which is truly healthy. So there is a significant difference and considerable distinction between the Book of our Lord and the Sunnah of our Prophet Muhammad, may Allaah's praise and salutations be upon him, and the expressions and statements found in the work *((Zaad al-Mustaqna')07-01)* or other similar books of fiqh. The Lord of Glory says in His Noble book, ❴*And We have indeed made the Qur'aan easy to understand and remember; then is there anyone who will remember?*❵-(Surah Qamar:17) Our Prophet Muhammad, may Allaah's praise and salutations be upon him, said, *{I was sent with the straightforward way of worshiping of Allaah Alone.}* [4]. And he said, *{Certainly, this religion is one of simplicity.}* [5]. As knowledge is something simple, and it is the differences that have occurred between the scholars that have preoccupied the students of knowledge away from study of the Book of Allaah and the Sunnah of the Messenger of Allaah, may Allaah's praise and salutations be upon him. Rather, it has even caused some of them to become supporters of separate factions or divisive groups. How excellent is the one who stated:

---

[4]    Narrated in Musnad Imaam Ahmad: 21788/ -on the authority of  Abu Amaamah Sidee Ibn 'Ajlaan. It was declared authentic by Sheikh al-Albaanee in Silsilat al-Hadeeth as-Saheehah: 2924.

[5]    Narrated in Saheeh al-Bukhaaree: 39/ Sunan an-Nasaa'ee: 5037/ -on the authority of Abu Hurairah. It was declared authentic by Sheikh al-Albaanee in Silsilat al-Hadeeth as-Saheehah: 1161, Mishkaat al-Masaabeh: 1246, Saheeh al-Jaame'a as-Sagheer: 1611, as well as in Saheeh Sunan an-Nasaa'ee.

*If it was not for the worldly rivalry and competition,*

*there would not be such books of debating like*

*al-Mughnee or al-Amad,*

*they legitimize their efforts by claiming to resolve complexities,*

*yet by what resulted, the problem of complexity only increased!*

So through this blessed way of study Allaah may bring benefit in a short period of time, because it is connected to and based upon the Book of Allaah and the Sunnah of the Messenger of Allaah, may Allaah's praise and salutations be upon him. And we discussed the subject of the censure of blind following in the book *((Establishing the Proof of the Misguidance of 'Abdur-Rahman at-Tahaan)11-22).* Therefore the religion is taken from the Book of Allaah and from the Sunnah of the Messenger of Allaah, may Allaah's praise and salutations be upon him. As for foremost relying upon the statements of this person and that person, and their differences, such that if you follow the Shaafa'ee school of jurisprudence then you consider something to be permissible, while if you were to follow the Hanafee or Hanbalee schools of jurisprudence then you would say that same thing is not permissible This itself is evidence that this concept of restricted closed schools of jurisprudence is something foreign that has infiltrated our understanding of the religion. As the Lord of Might and Glory says in His Noble Book, ❖*Do they not then consider the Qur'aan carefully? Had it been from other than Allaah, they would surely have found therein many contradictions*❖-(Surah an-Nisa'a:82) The Book of our Lord, and the Sunnah of our Prophet Muhammad, may Allaah's praise and salutations be upon him, do not contain contradictions. Rather the differences are from the understanding held by the people of knowledge, and some of the false inclinations and prejudices of a few of the people of knowledge.

Lastly, as for those scholars whom the majority of their speech comes from the Book of Allaah and the Sunnah, then these are those like Imaam al-Bukhaaree and Imaam Ahmad Ibn Hanbal, and Ibn Hazm, while being aware of his misconceptions in the area of belief, and Ibn Qayyim, Muhammad Isma'eel al-Ameer, as well as the likes of ash-Shawkaanee. And all praise is due to Allaah, there are indeed those scholars who the majority of their statements are taken from the Book of Allaah and the Sunnah. Therefore one feels comfortable and confident regarding them and the Muslims from the east and west of this earth have benefited from them.

*[FROM 'EXCELLENT RESPONSES TO QUESTIONS FROM THOSE PRESENT AND THOSE ABSENT': PAGE 237]*

# (11)

QUESTION: WHAT IS THE ISLAMIC RULING ON THE USE OF THE TELEVISION IF WE HAVE ISLAMIC DIALOGUES WITH THE CHRISTIANS, AND KNOWLEDGE BASED LECTURES THAT ARE SPECIFICALLY EDUCATIONAL OR CULTURAL?

nswer: As for the television, then it is essential that it not be brought into the home, as it involves worthless speech and music. Moreover, it involves the making of images of living beings and the Messenger of Allaah, may Allaah's praise and salutations be upon him, said, as is found in the two well known 'Saheeh' hadeeth collections from the hadeeth of Abu Talhah, *{The angels to not enter a house in which there is a dog or images.}* [1]. He also refused to enter the room of 'Aishah when he saw that there was a curtain upon which there where figures of living beings. So 'Aishah quickly said, "*I repent to Allaah.*" Then the Messenger of Allaah, may Allaah's praise and salutations be upon him and his family, took the curtain and tore it into separate pieces. Also, when he saw two cushions that had images upon them he said, *{Oh 'Aisha! The most severely punished people on the Day of Judgment are those who make such images.}* [2]. And one might say, [This prohibition only applies to three dimensional images.] However the figures mentioned, these being upon a garment, were not three dimensional. Imaam Ahmad narrated in his hadeeth collection "al-Musnad" on the authority of Jaabir, may Allaah be pleased with him, that *{the Prophet, may Allaah's praise and salutations be upon him and his family, when he entered the Ka'bah the day of the conquest of Mecca, found that there were images upon the walls*

---

[1]    Narrated in Saheeh al-Bukhaaree: 3225, 3322, 4002/ Saheeh Muslim: 2106/ Jaame'a at-Tirmidhee: 2804/Sunan an-Nasaa'ee: 4387, 5349, 5350/ Sunan Ibn Maajah: 3649/ & Musnad Imaam Ahmad: 15934, 27064/-on the authority of Abu Talhah al-Ansaaree. And it is in Saheeh Muslim: 2104/ Sunan Ibn Maajah: 3651/ & Musnad Imaam Ahmad: 24576/-on the authority of 'Aishah. And it is in Saheeh Muslim: 2105/ Sunan Abu Dawud: 4157/ Sunan an-Nasaa'ee: 4281/ & Musnad Imaam Ahmad: 26260/-on the authority of Umm al-Mu'mineen Maymoonah. And it is in Sunan an-Nasaa'ee: 4286/ Sunan Ibn Maajah: 3650/ & Musnad Imaam Ahmad: 8177/ Sunan ad-Daaramee: 2663/ -on the authority of 'Alee Ibn Abee Taalib. It was declared authentic by Sheikh al-Albaanee in Ghaayat al-Maraam 118, Saheeh at-Targheeb at-Tarheeb: 3058, 3058, 3103, as well as in his verification of the four "Sunan".

[2]    Narrated in Saheeh al-Bukhaaree: 6109/ Saheeh Muslim: 2107/Sunan an-Nasaa'ee: 5358, 5359, 5365/ & Musnad Imaam Ahmad: 24015, 24035/-on the authority of 'Aishah. It was declared authentic by Sheikh al-Albaanee in Ghaayat al-Maraam 118, Saheeh at-Targheeb at-Tarheeb: 3053, 3055, Mishkaat al-Masaabeh: 119, & Saheeh al-Jaame'a as-Sagheer: 2204, 5892.

*of the Ka'bah. There were images of Ibraheem and Isma'eel divining by arrows. So he called for a rag which was wet with water and wiped them away}.* This is evidence that the images referred to do not have to be that which has a physical form or is three dimensional.

Additionally, television involves worthless speech and music. It is narrated in Saheeh of Imaam al-Bukhaaree on the authority of Abu Aamar al-'Asharee that the Prophet, may Allaah's praise and salutations be upon him and his family, said, *{There will be a people from my Ummah who will make permissible fornication, dressing in silk, intoxicants, and musical instruments.}* [3]. Television also involves the practice of men looking at women if the announcer or broadcaster is a woman, or the practice of women looking at men if the announcer or broadcaster is a man. This is also something prohibited. Allaah, the Most High, the Most exalted says, ❧*Tell the believing men to lower their gaze (from looking at forbidden things), and protect their private parts (from illegal sexual acts, etc.). That is purer for them.*❧-(Surah an-Nur:30) And He says, ❧*And tell the believing women to lower their gaze from looking at forbidden things, and protect their private parts from illegal sexual acts*❧-(Surah an-Nur:31). In addition to this, is what is narrated by Imaams al-Bukhaaree and Muslim in their 'Saheeh' collections of hadeeth on the authority of Abu Hurairah, may Allaah be pleased with him, that the Prophet, may Allaah's praise and salutations be upon him and his family, said, *{Allaah has written for every son of Aadam a portion of adultery which a man will indulge in without escaping from it, and the adultery of the eye is the lustful look.}* -(al-Bukhaaree: 6243/ Muslim: 2657). Similarly, many periodicals and newspapers also have such immoral images, as well as promoting concepts that are foreign and unacceptable in Islaam. Therefore that which I advise the

---

[3]    Narrated in Saheeh al-Bukhaaree is a mu'alaq narration after hadeeth 5590/ -on the authority of  Abu Maalik al-'Asha'ree. It was declared authentic by Sheikh al-Albaanee in Silsilat al-Hadeeth as-Saheehah: 91

Muslim who truly wants to receive news, is to suffice himself with the use of a radio. But also to listen to the news from the radio while being aware that these broadcasters are liars and deceivers As whenever I was able to do so, from the beginning of the Gulf crisis up until this very day, I listened to the radio after salaatul-Isha. But all that I heard were deceptions, hypocrisy, deceit, and repeated statements. So we strongly disapprove and censure this worthless speech. And from Allaah we seek assistance.

*[FROM A DEFENDING MISSION FROM AUDIO LECTURES UPON THE PEOPLE OF IGNORANCE & SOPHISTRY: VOL.2, PAGE 468]*

# (12)

QUESTION: WHAT IS THE ISLAMIC RULING ON READING DAILY NEWSPAPERS, PUBLICATIONS, OR MAGAZINES FOR THE PURPOSE OF GETTING SOCIETAL, ISLAMIC, GOVERNMENTAL, OR CULTURAL NEWS IN ORDER TO UNDERSTAND WHAT IS GOING ON AROUND US?

nswer: That which I advise you is to stay far away from this, as the majority of these newspapers and magazines simply serve the different governments, and deceive and mislead people for the sake of these governments. But let us say that there was indeed a newspaper or a magazine that conveyed the truth. Even after this, every individual only has a limited amount of time to be wasted on this newspaper or magazine. Yet in this 'news' we only see distressing thoughts and statements, and we see in it that which can only lead one to worry and anxiety. Also, perhaps there may be the publishing of insults to Islaam, the criticism of the Muslims, and similar things. But in any case we do not say that it is prohibited to read them; however, we advise the student of knowledge to content himself with the Book of Allaah and the Sunnah, as-

*The truly important news is never fails to reach everyone.*

*News reaches you from the one who you did not expect.*

So important news does not hide itself it spreads as quickly as possible throughout the entire area! As for those magazines related to atheist methodologies and concepts, then it is expected that they only promote misconceptions and doubts while causing you to waste your time. Additionally, those managing these various forms of the electronic media and those responsible for the production of newspapers are usually people known to practice deception and hypocrisy. And from Allaah we seek help and assistance.

*[FROM 'A DEFENDING MISSION FROM AUDIO LECTURES UPON THE PEOPLE OF IGNORANCE AND SOPHISTRY': VOL.2, PAGE 467]*

# *(13)*

QUESTION: LASTLY, WHAT IS YOUR ADVICE TO US AS TO HOW TO SEEK KNOWLEDGE? ALSO WHICH BOOKS AND TAPES ARE NEEDED BY THE BEGINNING STUDENT OF KNOWLEDGE?

nswer: That which I advise is that he correspond and communicate with the people of knowledge, and that if he has the ability to travel to them that he does so. By this it meant the likes of Sheikh al-Albaanee, Sheikh Ibn Baaz, Sheikh 'Abdul-Muhsin al-'Abaad, Sheikh Rabee'a Ibn Haadee, and Sheikh al-'Utheimeen. Again, if one is able to travel to them he should do so, and if not them he should keep in contact them by means of the telephone and sending of letters. And if there are any eminent scholars found in his own land then we advise him to gather around them. As well as to invite the people to gather around them, with the condition that they do not become a blind bigoted supporter nor someone of group partisanship and division. Certainly the bigoted supporter only calls to his affiliated group or his restricted path, and Allaah has said: ❁*Surely, the religion is for Allaah only*❁-(Surah Zumar: 3). So purity of intention for the religion and in calling to Allaah the Most High, the Most exalted is something required. Allaah says ❁*Let there arise out of you a group of people inviting to all that is good*❁-(Surah Aal-'Imraan:104), and ❁*This is my way; I invite unto Allaah with sure knowledge, I and whosoever follows me*❁-(Surah Yusuf:108), and ❁*Invite to the Way of your Lord with wisdom and fair preaching, and argue with them in a way that is better.*❁-(Surah an-Nahl:125). And here there is a matter that you must be forewarned against. This is that some of the people of group partisanship and division will probably swear to you that they are not a person upon partisanship and separation, but this is because they remain confused about this issue. But if they invite you to participate in elections. or you see them praising others who are known people of group partisanship, receiving, and meeting with them. Then know that he stands in a position of uncertainty and doubt, and it is proper that you be cautious in your dealings with him.

*[FROM 'EXCELLENT RESPONSES TO QUESTIONS FROM THOSE PRESENT AND THOSE ABSENT': PAGE 139]*

# (14)

QUESTION: SOME PEOPLE SAY TO THE STUDENTS OF KNOWLEDGE, "YOU ARE IDLE WITHOUT WORK." SO WHAT SHOULD OUR REPLY TO THIS BE?

nswer: The refutation against them is that the idler is the one who does not seek closeness to Allaah, the Most High, the Most Exalted through working and efforts. As for the student of knowledge, then he- all praise is due to Allaah, is one who is engaged in serving the religion of Islaam. And the Lord of Glory says in His noble book: ❁*Of every troop of them, a party only should go forth, that they who are left behind may get instructions in religion, and that they may warn their people when they return to them, so that they may beware of evil.*❁-(Surah Tawbah:122) The Prophet, Allaah's praise and salutations be upon him and his family, said as is found in the two Saheeh hadeeth collections from the hadeeth Mu'aweeyah, may Allaah be pleased with he: *{Whoever Allaah intends good for He grants him understanding in the religion}* [1]. And he said is is reported in Saheeh Muslim from the hadeeth of 'Umar, may Allaah be pleased with him: *{Allaah raised one people by this Book and lowers other people by it.}* [2].

The seeking of knowledge is considered from the best means of coming closer to Allaah, and the Muslims have a tremendous need for scholars, and this is an evident reality today, as well as for tomorrow and after tomorrow. Therefore, know that the students of knowledge are not from those who are squandering away their lives. The one who squanders his life is the regular drinker of alcohol, or the one who is occupied with movies and entertainment shows, or the one

[1]    Narrated in Saheeh al-Bukhaaree: 71, 3116, 7312/ Saheeh Muslim: 1037/ Sunan Ibn Maajah: 221/ al-Muwatta Maalik: 1300, 1667/ Musnad Imaam Ahmad: 16395: 16404, and other narrations/ Musannaf Ibn Abee Shaybah: 31792/ & Sunan ad-Daaramee: 224, 226/- on the authority of Mu'aweeyah. And it is found in Jaame'a al-Tirmidhee: 2645/ & Musnad Imaam Ahmad: 2786/ & Sunan ad-Daaramee: 270, 2706/- on the authority of Ibn "Abbaas. And  it is found in Sunan Ibn Maajah: 220/ Musannaf 'Abdul-Razzaaq: 30851/- on the authority of Abu Hurairah. It was declared authentic by Sheikh al-Albaanee in Saheeh al-Aadab al-Mufrad: 517, Silsilat al-Hadeeth as-Saheehah: 1194, 1195, 1196, Saheeh at-Targheeb at-Tarheeb: 67, as well as in other of his books. Sheikh Muqbil declared it authentic in al-Jaame'a al-Saheeh: 9, 3123, 4650.

[2]    Narrated in Saheeh Muslim: 817/ Sunan Ibn Maajah: 218/ & Musnad Imaam Ahmad: 233/ Sunan ad-Daaramee: 3360/-on the authority of 'Umar Ibn al-Khattab. It was declared authentic by Sheikh al-Albaanee in Silsilat al-Hadeeth as-Saheehah: 2239, Mishkaat al-Masaabeh: 2115, & Saheeh al-Jaame'a as-Sagheer: 1896.

whose focus is watching or playing football or soccer, or the one always hanging around in the streets, and the one who is dedicated to musical and idle pleasures. But as for the student of knowledge he perseveres night and day, as truly seeking knowledge is a tremendous hardship. The student of knowledge is incredibly fatigued from being busy all day long hurriedly going back and forth in this effort. Thus this demands patience as was stated by 'Abdullah Ibn 'Umar when he said to a student of knowledge: "*You should obtain two shoes made of iron.*" Additionally, it was mentioned by Yahya Ibn Abee Kather, may Allaah The Most High have mercy upon him: "*Knowledge cannot be achieved through ease and comfort of one's body*"

Therefore it is not proper that you listen and comply with those of your fathers who scheme regarding you or others who devise similar plans. As Allaah the Most high and Most Exalted, says in His Noble Book: *❧Obey not him whose heart We have made heedless of Our remembrance, one who follows his own lusts and whose affair -deeds has been lost.❧*-(Surah Kahf:28) And Allaah the Most High, the Most Exalted says in His Noble Book: *❧Therefore withdraw from him who turns away from Our Reminder and desires nothing but the life of this world. That is what they could reach of knowledge.❧*-(Surah an-Najm:29-30) *❧They know only the outside appearance of the life of the world, and they are heedless of the Hereafter❧*-(Surah ar-Rum: 7) So you deficient one, oh deficient one! Do you not know that the Prophet, prayers and good mention be upon him and his family, said: *{When a son of Aadam dies his deeds end except for three matters: a continuing charity, or a righteous child who supplicates for them, or knowledge by which others are benefited.}* [3]. Do you <u>want to facilitat</u>e your son becoming a drinker of alcohol, or

[3]   Narrated in Saheeh Muslim: 1631/ Sunan Abu Dawud: 2880/ Jaame'a at-Tirmidhee: 1376/ Sunan an-Nasaa'ee: 3681/ Musnad Imaam Ahmad: 8627/ & Sunan ad-Daaramee: 559/-on the authority of Abu Hurairah. It was declared authentic by Sheikh al-Albaanee in Saheeh at-Targheeb at-Tarheeb: 78, 93, Mishkaat al-Masaabeh: 127, 203, & Saheeh al-Jaame'a as-Sagheer: 793, and the three 'Sunan' collections

a homosexual, or a communist, or a Ba'athee socialist, or a Christian?!? *Verily, it is not the eyes that grow blind, but it is the hearts which are in the breasts that grow blind.*-(Surah al-Hajj:46)  As your son if you do not ensure that he receives an Islamic education, then you can be viewing him as someone who is simple minded. And so due to this lack of education maybe he will eventually  come to  strike you upon your face, as well as strike your back. Yet if you had educated him with a proper Islamic education, then he would fear Allaah, the One free of all faults and Most Exalted. And he would know that Allaah, glorified and exalted said: *And your Lord has decreed that you worship none but Him. And that you be dutiful to your parents.*-(Surah al-Isra: 23)

And he would know that the pleasure of his Lord is to be found in pleasing his parents, the anger of his Lord is gained through angering his parents and that disobedience to ones parents is from the most serious of major sins. However, if you wipe out his perception and comprehension of such matters, and maybe he may become an alcoholic, or become a military general obsessed by acquiring more stars of higher rank. But if you have twenty stars to show your high rank and you have not established that which Allaah has made obligatory upon you then you are foolish.  Allaah, the Most Perfect, the Most High says: *Let not the free disposal and affluence of the disbelievers throughout the land deceive you. A brief enjoyment; then, their ultimate abode is Hell; and worst indeed is that place for rest.*-(Surah Aal-'Imraan:196,197). It is upon you to fear Allaah, and to be diligent in guiding your sons towards seeking knowledge and to spend your wealth on your sons for this purpose. As assuredly if your son said to you: "*I will go to America to complete my education*", then some of the people would probably assist their sons by giving them 100 thousand riyals or an even greater amount! While saying: "*Go my son and complete your education so that you may return*". However after this "education" their thinking and beliefs will be corrupted and become that of a secularist, or Ba'athist socialist, or a communist, or some other brand of the various ideologies. And we have a cassette regarding this subject by the name: "*My Advice to Fathers & Mothers*"

*[FROM 'BRIDLING THE RESISTANT ONE': PAGE 590]*

# (15)

QUESTION: WHAT IS THE RULING REGARDING THE ONE WHO DOES NOT OBEY HIS MOTHER IN THE ISSUE OF SEEKING KNOWLEDGE IF SHE WILL NOT GIVE HIM PERMISSION TO GO TO ANOTHER LAND TO SEEK KNOWLEDGE? IS HE CONSIDERED FROM THOSE WHO HAVE FALLEN INTO A MAJOR SIN AS SOMEONE WHO BEHAVED BADLY TOWARD HIS PARENTS? OR IS HE FROM THOSE WHO ARE REWARDED FOR HIS SEEKING KNOWLEDGE EVEN THOUGHT HE DISOBEYED HIS MOTHER IN CONFORMANCE WITH THE STATEMENT OF THE MESSENGER (UPON HIM BE GOOD MENTION AND PEACE), "THERE IS NO OBEDIENCE TO THE CREATION IN DISOBEDIENCE TO THE CREATOR."?

nswer: He should obey his mother if she had a need for him to financially support for or as a need for him to serve her and she does not have anyone else to do so. But if she does not require either one of these, and he does not fear for her that she would grieve and cry to a degree that it would harm her eyesight or cry and grieve so much that her mind would be harmed, that it is not required to obey her. Because seeking knowledge is an obligation and the Messenger, may Allaah's praise and salutations be upon him and his family, said:*{ Obedience is in that which is permissible and good.}* [1]. Imaam Ahmad mention this as was transmitted from him by Ibn Haanee and which we've also transmitted from him in the book *((Makhraj min al-Fitnah)11-21).*

*[FROM 'A DEFENDING MISSION FROM AUDIO LECTURES UPON THE PEOPLE OF IGNORANCE & SOPHISTRY': VOL. 1, PAGE 437]*

[1]    Narrated in Saheeh al-Bukhaaree: 7145, 7257/ Saheeh Muslim: 1840/ Sunan Abu Dawud: 2625/  Sunan an-Nasaa'ee: 4210/ Musnad Imaam Ahmad: 623,726, 1021/ -on the authority of 'Alee Ibn Abee Taalib. It was declared authentic by Sheikh al-Albaanee in Silsilat al-Hadeeth as-Saheehah: 181, Mishkaat al-Masaabeh: 3665, & Saheeh al-Jaame'a as-Sagheer: 7319, 7519, and in his verification of al-'Emaan by Ibn Taymeeyah.

# (16)

QUESTION: WHICH OF THEM HAS PRECEDENCE: GOING FORTH IN SEEKING KNOWLEDGE OR GOING FORTH FOR JIHAAD? ADDITIONALLY, IS IT REQUIRED TO GET PERMISSION FROM YOUR PARENTS IN BOTH SITUATIONS?

nswer: As for asked related to jihaad then it is a requirement, as is found narration of 'Abdullah Ibn 'Amr, may Allaah be pleased with them both, that *{the Prophet saw a man who intended to go forth in jihaad so he said to him: "Are your parents were alive?" He responded: "Yes." The Prophet then said: "Then strive through serving them."}* [1]. This narration is found in the 'Saheeh' collections of Imaams al-Bukhaaree and Muslim. As for seeking knowledge that if they both have a need for you to support them or to serve them or both of them are advancing age and they do not have anyone else who would serve them, then is upon you to give precedence to them. And Allaah will make for you a means of escape or way out from that situation. As perhaps Allaah will facilitate for you one who would teach you in your home or in your land. However if your parents do not have a need for you to support them, being self-sufficient financially. And I do not intend by "self-sufficient financially" this is what is commonly known as being rich, but that they possess what is sufficient for them from sufficient food and drink. Then it is not required to seek their permission.

Also, perhaps your father may be a communist or someone who's deficient in his religion. So if you said to him: "*I'm going to work in Saudi Arabia.*" He would say: "*This is good my son.*" But if you were to say to him: "*I am going forth to seek knowledge.*" He would say: "*No!*" raise his voice and your mother might do likewise. Therefore there is no obedience to them in this case, as the Prophet, upon him and his family be Allaah's praises and the best of salutations, said:*{ Obedience is in that which is permissible and good.}* [2].

[1]    Narrated in Saheeh al-Bukhaaree: 3004/ Saheeh Muslim: 2539/ Sunan an-Nasaa'ee: 3105/ Musnad Imaam Ahmad: 6508, 6726/ -on the authority of 'Abdullah Ibn 'Amr. It was declared authentic by Sheikh al-Albaanee in Irwa' al-Ghaleel: 1199, Ghaayat al-Maraam 281, & Saheeh at-Targheeb at-Tarheeb: 2480, 2483.

[2]    Narrated in Saheeh al-Bukhaaree: 7145, 7257/ Saheeh Muslim: 1840/ Sunan Abu Dawud: 2625/ Sunan an-Nasaa'ee: 4210/ Musnad Imaam Ahmad: 623,726, 1021/ -on the authority of 'Alee Ibn Abee Taalib. It was declared authentic by Sheikh al-Albaanee in Silsilat al-Hadeeth as-Saheehah: 181, Mishkaat al-Masaabeh: 3665, & Saheeh al-Jaame'a as-Sagheer: 7319, 7519, and in his verification of al-'Emaan by Ibn Taymeeyah.

And this is what was mentioned by Imaam Ahmad as is found in the book *((al-Masa'il)07-28)* transmitted by Ibn Haanee, as Imaam Ahmad was asked about this issue in regard to seeking knowledge.

*[FROM 'BRIDLING THE RESISTANT ONE': PAGE 419]*

# *(17)*

QUESTION: HOW SHOULD THE STUDENT OF KNOWLEDGE BEHAVE TOWARDS HIS PARENT WHO ATTEMPTS TO PREVENT HIM FROM SEEKING KNOWLEDGE?

nswer: He should deal with them gently and with mildness and say to them: The Prophet, upon him and his family be Allaah's praises and the best of salutations, said: *{When a son of Aadam dies his deeds end except for three matters:..}* and from them is *{...a righteous child who supplicates for him}* [1]. And the Lord of Might has said in His Book: *And those who believe and whose offspring follow them in Faith, to them shall We join their offspring, and We shall not decrease the reward of their deeds in anything. Every person is a pledge for that which he has earned.*-(Surah at-Tur: 21) and he said: *And those who say: "Our Lord! Bestow on us from our wives and our offspring who will be the comfort of our eyes, and make us leaders for the pious*-(Surah al-Furqan:74).

So it is required for them to praise Allaah the Exalted that their child is not an alcoholic, or a homosexual, or a fornicator, or one who behaves badly towards them. Exhort and remind your parents of these things so that they will agree. But if they still refuse then go forth to study and afterwards write and speak with them and treat them well as much as you can. And if Allaah wishes then He will guide them through the child, as how many fathers forbad their sons initially, and then after some days perhaps the father himself comes himself to study with us, when he saw the behavior of his son and his good treatment towards him.

*[FROM 'A DEFENDING MISSION FROM AUDIO LECTURES UPON THE PEOPLE OF IGNORANCE & SOPHISTRY': VOL. 2, PAGE 378]*

---

[1] Narrated in Saheeh Muslim: 1631/ Sunan Abu Daawud: 2880/ Jaame'a at-Tirmidhee: 1376/ Sunan an-Nasaa'ee: 3681/ Musnad Imaam Ahmad: 8627/ & Sunan ad-Daaramee: 559/ -on the authority of Abu Hurairah. It was declared authentic by Sheikh al-Albaanee in Saheeh at-Targheeb at-Tarheeb: 78, 93, Mishkaat al-Masaabeh: 127,203, & Saheeh al-Jaame'a as-Sagheer: 793 as well as in his verification of the three 'Sunan'.

# *(18)*

QUESTION: WHY IS IT NOT A CONDITION TO GET PERMISSION FROM YOUR PARENTS WHEN GOING TO SEEK KNOWLEDGE, BUT REQUIRED WHEN GOING FOR JIHAAD? ISN'T THERE A DISTINCTION IN THIS, THAT IF THEY HAVE A NEED FOR YOU THAT YOU DO NOT GO FOR KNOWLEDGE, AND IF THEY DO NOT HAVE A NEED FOR YOU THEN YOU MAY GO SEEK KNOWLEDGE?

nswer: Certainly, is has a necessary distinction and that distinction has been explained. As for jihaad in the path of Allaah it is a collective general obligation, whereas seeking knowledge is an individual obligation, seeking knowledge is an obligation upon every Muslim. And we specify that knowledge which is an individual obligation as that matters which you as an individual utilize in your worship and that which it is necessary for you to understand, such as the correct fundamental beliefs, how to pray the obligatory prayers, what obligatory charity you must give if you possess the required amount of wealth, and the obligatory pilgrimage once you have decided to make that pilgrimage, the regulations of buying and selling if this is your profession, and the regulations of jihaad in the path of Allaah if you have decided to undertake it. Therefore seeking knowledge is an obligation upon every Muslim.

[FROM 'BRIDLING THE RESISTANT ONE': PAGE 219]

# *(19)*

QUESTION: ESTEEMED SHEIKH, MAY ALLAAH PRESERVE YOU, WE HOPE THAT YOU WOULD GIVE ADVICE TO YOUR SONS FROM AMONG THE STUDENTS OF KNOWLEDGE WHO LIVE IN ABU DHABEE AND THE UNITED ARAB EMIRATES AS A WHOLE.

nswer: That which I advise our brothers with a seriousness and diligence in acquiring beneficial knowledge, and that they do not busy themselves with that which does not truly help them. As differing and the separation arises from the lack of activity. It is said: so-and-so scholar is correct, and so-and-so scholar is wrong, and that so-and-so scholar you should not take knowledge from him, and for so-and-so scholar is such and such. So I say: it is obligatory that you say to yourself that you will be like the example of so-and-so scholar or even better than him otherwise the only thing you will end up with is occupying yourself with is the going from this masjid to that masjid, and from this sitting to this other sitting with *"So-and-so scholar is correct and this other one is mistaken."*. Rather I advise you to be serious and diligent and likewise if it is easy upon you to travel; then if you are informed that in such and such place some of the brothers are benefiting, then it is fitting that you travel to them and benefit from them.

We also advise them towards to spread the Book of Allaah and the Sunnah of Messenger of Allaah, upon him and his family be Allaah's praises and the best of salutations, upon the understanding of the first generations, and to visit their brothers from the people of knowledge. And we advise them to seek out scholars from the scholars of the land of the two Holy sanctuaries and Najd as well those from any other lands. Additionally, to be with the general people who are 'Sunni' in order that they may explain to them the methodology of the people of the Sunnah. Also having lectures has benefit and an effect upon the people, all praise is due to Allaah the mighty. However the effect of individual lectures, it is not of the same degree of benefit as regularly held lessons. And all praise is due to Allaah Lord of all the worlds.

*[FROM 'A DEFENDING MISSION FROM AUDIO LECTURES UPON THE PEOPLE OF IGNORANCE & SOPHISTRY': VOL. 2-PAGE 103]*

# *(20)*

QUESTION: OH ABU 'ABDUR-RAHMAN, WE NEED FOR YOU TO INFORM US HOW YOU ORGANIZE YOUR TIME IN SEEKING KNOWLEDGE. WHEN DO YOU DO YOUR RESEARCH, WHEN DO YOU TEACH YOUR BROTHERS, AND HOW MANY LESSONS DO YOU HAVE DURING A DAY AND A NIGHT?  AND WE ASK ALLAAH FOR SINCERITY OF INTENTION FOR YOU AND FOR OURSELVES.

nswer: At present, after salatul-fajr I review the research related writings of my brothers which they hope to publish. Then a short while before the sun rise above the horizon, I go to an open area for a while to rest and recuperate my energy. Then a little while after the sun rises, we read from *((as-Saheeh al-Musnad Memaa Lasaa fee as-Saheehayn)02-35)*. Afterwards, we proceed to the library for research until the call to prayer of salatul-dhuhr. After the call to prayer of salatul-dhuhr we study from *((Tafseer Ibn Katheer)01-01)* or something related to the study of the proper recognition of dictation or to handwriting. Then after salatul-dhuhr, lunch, and the essential period of resting, if I have not done less than usual then I am not able to study more. So then I rest a while from that time until the time of salutul-asr. At that time, I go to the masjid for salutul-asr, and afterwards I teach from *((Saheeh al-Bukhaaree)02-01)*. Then after that lesson I instruct some of the brothers in the study of *((Sharh of Ibn Aqeel)10-06)*. After this lesson, depending on the time remaining, I rest until the sun sets then I make wudhu and proceed to the masjid. After salatul-maghrib I teach from *((Saheeh Muslim)02-02)*, and after salatul-isha I teach from the work *((as-Sunnah)06-22)* by 'Abdullah Ibn Ahmad Ibn Hanbal.

As for the research that I am presently working on, it is the study of *((Mustadraak of al-Haakim)02-25)*, and I am on the verge of completing it. In this I am examining all the hadeeth narrations which he declared where authentic, or in which there is possible disagreement regarding due to the possibility of error from al-Hakim when he states: "*Authentic according to the conditions held by the Imaams Bukhaaree and Muslim*", or "*Authentic according to the conditions of Imaam Muslim*". So I am investigating these and I consider those error that are considered to be from the mistakes of Imaam Haakim not from the errors of Imaam adh-Dhahabee in his review of the work, may Allaah have mercy upon him. Similarly, I am working on the book *((Hadeeth Narrations that have Hidden defects but which upon only a basic examination are considered authentic)02-36)*. The after some days, if Allaah wills, I will return to my work upon *((as-Saheeh al-Musnad Memaa Lasaa fee as-Saheehayn)02-35)*, when I have finished these other endeavors, Allaah wiling. In any case my time in these days is quite restricted, due the increased numbers of students. So I am not satisfied with the little time that remains to be given to my research. Yet on the other hand, in the beginning of my efforts there where only a few brothers; so that the majority of my time was able to be spent in research. And all praise is due to Allaah that resulted in tremendous good.

So I advise my brothers who are students of knowledge to study the life histories of 'Abdullah Ibn Mubaarak, Imaam Ahmad, Imaam al-Bukhaaree and Imaam Muslim, as well as those who adhered to and followed their path from the scholars of hadeeth- until you understand how to preserve your time. As I am not completely satisfied with my own efforts nor how I have been able to proceed, so the objective has not been realized completely nor fallen short of entirely. And all praise is due to Allaah, certainly a great deal of good has come forth from what was accomplished.

And I have forgotten to mention an important matter, that being the editing and correction of material that was previously only distributed on cassette tapes. We had spread tremendous good through these audio tapes, and they were received and well accepted by the students of knowledge. And some of them were prepared and willing to examine what those lectures contained and indicate any mistakes or errors, then correct the material of the tape as was required. So than after that stage, I further corrected them after the material was transcribed, and then these works were released. And there have come from these efforts tremendous benefit. The book *((al-Fawaakahu al-Jannah)12-34)* was produced from some previous lectures, as well as the book *((al-Muqtarah)04-23)*; it being questions and answers related to hadeeth sciences and terminology. In addition the book *((Qirat al-'Ayn fee Ajweebat Qad'ed al-'Alaabee*

126

*wa Saahib al-'Adeen)12-18)*, the book *((al-Qawl al-'Ameen fee Bayaan Fadhaaeh al-Mudhabdhabeen)12-40)* the book *((Maqatil as-Sheikh Jameel are-Rahman)12-35),* rahimhu Allaahu ta'ala", the book *((al-Masaar'at)12-36)* as well as a work composed of rulings in various matters which is named *((Ijaabatul-Saa'el 'An Ahemul Masaa'el)07-15),*and the book *((Qamaa' al-Ma'aanid wa Zujur al-Haaqid al-Haasid)07-16)* which encompasses various subject related to the situations that we find ourselves dealing with in present age. Issues and subjects such as voting and elections, and such as the issue of the many divisive groups of partisanship. As cassette tape is only a medium, which just like an individual- can considered foolish and ignorant, or otherwise.

In general, I hope that Allaah will bring benefit through these cassette lectures. And all praise is due to Allaah, they are easy and simple to benefit from, and the common people certainly have a need for their share of our efforts to call to the truth. So if we come to a common person and we say to him: *"Waleed Ibn Muslim is a 'mudallis' in hadeeth narrations and Ibn Laheeyah is 'mukhtalat', and Sha'bee did not hear naarations from Umm Salamah."*; then he will nor understand what we are saying in the least and you are only wasting his time. On account of this we are eager to distribute these general audio cassettes. However this can occur after giving them proper attention and review, and that is the result of having the time, to give to it. But I am not an individual to be followed in this, as I am not satisfied with myself, by Allaah I am not truly satisfied with myself. As sometimes I will lose some of my time with the small children. As I myself have made mistakes in this, due to many problems that have reached me. Because of this, a person himself might simply sit down in the place of children to sometimes only play and joke with them.

*[ FROM 'A DEFENDING MISSION FROM AUDIO LECTURES UPON THE PEOPLE OF IGNORANCE & SOPHISTRY': VOL. 1, PAGE 472]*

# (21)

QUESTION: THERE ARE MANY HADEETH NARRATIONS WHICH ARE ADDRESSED TO "BELIEVERS" OR "MUSLIMS" WITHOUT USING THE PHRASE "WOMAN" (OR WOMEN). DOES THIS INDICATE THAT THE MUSLIM "WOMAN" IS NOT INTENDED BY THESE SPECIFIC TEXTS, AS THERE ARE OTHER VERSES OF THE QUR'AAN AND HADEETH NARRATIONS WHICH DO SPECIFICALLY MENTION THEM AND ARE DIRECTED TOWARDS EXPLAINING THE RULINGS FOR WOMEN AND CLARIFYING THEM?

nswer: The fundamental rule is that the entire Sharee'ah generally applies to everyone, male and female, just as Allaah, the Most Glorified and the Most Exalted, states in His Noble Book, *Never will I allow to be lost the work of any of you, be he male or female. You are one of another*-(Surah Aal-'Imraan:195)  So the fundamental rule is that the entire Sharee'ah generally applies to everyone. There is nothing specified to just men except those matters which there is exact evidence for that specification, and there is nothing specified to just women except those matters which there is exact evidence for that specification.

Indeed, some women came and mentioned to the Messenger, may Allaah's praise and salutations be upon him, that indeed Muslim men engage in jihaad, and that Allaah, the Most Perfect and the Most High mentions men in verses but not women. Then this verse was revealed, *Never will I allow to be lost the work of any of you, be he male or female. You are one of another*-(Surah Aal-'Imraan:195)    And Allaah, the Most High, also revealed, *Indeed, the Muslim men and Muslim women, the believing men and believing women, the obedient men and obedient women, the truthful men and truthful women, the patient men and patient women, the humble men and humble women, the charitable men and charitable women, the fasting men and fasting women, the men who guard their private parts and the women who do so, and the men who remember Allah often and the women who do so...*-(Surah al-Ahzaab:35) until the end of the verse. So the fundamental rule is that the entire Sharee'ah applies generally to all except where it specifies one gender.

*[FROM 'A DEFENDING MISSION FROM AUDIO LECTURES UPON THE PEOPLE OF IGNORANCE & SOPHISTRY': VOL. 2, PAGE 459]*

# (22)

QUESTION: WHAT IS THE SHAREE'AH
KNOWLEDGE THAT IT IS OBLIGATORY
UPON A WOMAN TO LEARN?

nswer: First, it is obligatory upon her to learn her fundamental beliefs from the Book and the Sunnah, and then her ritual prayers, knowing how exactly the Messenger of Allaah, may Allaah's praise and salutation be upon him and his family, prayed. If she is someone who possesses wealth she must learn what Allaah has made obligatory upon her from the obligatory charity or zakaat. If she is engaged in buying and selling she must learn the related rulings of that commerce. Likewise, if she is involved in any work, then it is obligatory upon her to learn the ruling related to that field or endeavor. This is what is meant by the hadeeth of the Messenger of Allaah, may Allaah's praise and salutation be upon him and his family, *{Seeking knowledge is an obligation upon every Muslim}* [1]. Similarly, if she is a female doctor it is obligatory upon her to study the issues such as: is it permissible for her to mix with men, is it permissible to use as medication that contains forbidden substances? It is required that you understand the rulings of those matters related to the work you are engaged in from the guidance of the Book and the Sunnah. What I mean by this is that she gain an understanding of the relevant evidences from the Book and the Sunnah, not that she restrict herself to only those medical practices based upon the knowledge from the Book and the Sunnah.

*[FROM 'A DEFENDING MISSION FROM AUDIO LECTURES UPON THE PEOPLE OF IGNORANCE & SOPHISTRY': VOL. 2, PAGE 476]*

---

[1]   Narrated in Sunan Ibn Maajah: 224/ -on the authority of 'Anas Ibn Maalik. It was declared authentic by Sheikh al-Albaanee in Saheeh at-Targheeb at-Tarheeb: 72, Mishkaat al-Masaabeh: 218, Saheeh al-Jaame'a as-Sagheer: 3813, 3914, & Saheeh Sunan Ibn Maajah.

# (23)

QUESTION: ESTEEMED SHEIKH, IF OUR BROTHERS DESIRE BENEFICIAL KNOWLEDGE THEY GO TO YOU AND LEARN. BUT WE ARE YOUNG WOMEN WHO HAVE GREAT IGNORANCE OF THE AFFAIRS IN OUR RELIGION. SPECIFICALLY, WE NEED TO BE TAUGHT THE RULES OF HOW TO RECITE THE QUR'AAN; HOWEVER WE DO NOT HAVE THE ABILITY TO HAVE A TEACHER FOR THIS AMONG OURSELVES OR TO CONDUCT THESE LESSONS OURSELVES. SO HOW CAN WE SEEK BENEFICIAL KNOWLEDGE?

nswer: Allaah says, *And whosoever fears Allaah and keeps his duty to Him, He will make a way for him to get out from every difficulty. And He will provide him from sources he never could imagine.*-(Surah at-Talaq:2,3) and He says *So be afraid of Allaah; and Allaah teaches you. And Allaah is All-Knower of everything.*-(Surah al-Baqarah:287) and He says *Oh you who believe! If you obey and fear Allaah, He will grant you a criterion to judge between right and wrong*-(Surah al-Anfaal:29) and He says *Oh you who believe, Fear Allaah, and believe in His Messenger...* up until his statement, *...and He will give you a light by which you shall walk straight.*-(Surah al-Haadeed:28) Therefore if we fear Allaah, then Allaah the Most Glorified and the Most Exalted will facilitate for us those who will help teach us, and make easy for us acquiring that book which is beneficial and that audio tape which is beneficial. And I praise and thank Allaah the Most Glorified and the Most Exalted, that we have among us young women who have reached the level of having authored works, that by the blessing and grace of Allaah, are beneficial. And in the coming days if Allaah wills, such a book will be made available which is entitled: *((My Advice to Women)12-31)*. It is presently being printed. Another example is that recently a book has become available from a sister which is a work that I do not know any comparison to in its subject area, that being the area of studying the distinguished characteristics of the Prophet. As there is known to be a *((small treatise)09-09)* authored by Imaam at-Tirmidhee in this subject, and I was informed that Imaam al-Baghawee has authored a similar work, but I have not read it. But it is hoped that a copy will be sent to us from the land of the Two Holy Places. This new work is by the grace of Allaah, as another book like it has not been compiled with the objective of carefully selecting only authentic narrations. It will have a verse of the Qur'aan placed at the head of every chapter, and will be entitled either "al-Jama'ah as-Saheeh fe as-Shamail al-Muhammadeyyah" or *((as-Saheeh al-Musnad fe as-Shamail al-Muhammadeyyah)09-04).* When the book is completed it will be decided which of the two titles is more worthy. So the object of bringing up this issue is to point out how many students of knowledge have benefited simply from reviewing beneficial books individually. Therefore, if you are able you should have a library which contains such as: *((al-Lu'Lu wa' al-Marjaan feemaa Itifaq Aleeheh as-Sheikhayn)07-01)* and the work *((Bulugh al-Maraam)02-34)* and *((Nayl al-Awtaar)03-08), ((Fath al-Majeed Sharh Kitaab at-Tawheed)06-12),* and the book *((al-'Uluu)06-45)* by Hafidh ad-Dhahabee or its summarized version from Sheikh al-Albaanee. This is because books commonly make reference to other works as the source of something within them, so that a researcher will be using a book and it will say in it, *"narrated by at-Tabaranee".* Therefore he then needs to purchase the work *((Mu'jam al-Kabeer)02-21).* Or it may say *"narrated by al-Humaidee in his work Musnad,"* so that he then needs to purchase the work Musnad al-Humaidee. Indeed, at one time I possessed a library which was held in two or three large bookcases, and I used to think that my library contained the books of the world, until I was writing the work *((at-Talea'ah Fee Rad 'Alaa Gulaat as-Shee'ah)11-12).* As when I had composed part of it, it became clear that there were several reference works that I did not possess. Then I began compiling *((as-Saheeh al-Musnad Min Asbaab an-Nuzul)01-10)* and after working on this I again realized that my library required additional works as references. So a researcher will often come across references to other books such that he then says, *"I will go and buy this book."* Therefore I advise you, female students, to strive in acquiring knowledge, in acquiring beneficial books, and in the memorization of knowledge. So how excellent is your position if you were to sit in your home and memorize the Book of Allaah, and then memorize *((al-Lu'Lu wa' al-Marjaan feemaa Itifaq Aleeheh as-Sheikhayn)07-01)*, and memorize *((Riyadh as-Saaliheen)02-11)*! We are in true need of righteous women to establish the call to Allaah among the ranks of the women. There has entered among us evil matters that spread by way of some women. Indeed the enemies of Islaam have mislead her, lied to her, and deluded her, such that perhaps she comes to hold Islaam is disdain or contempt as a religion, and so washes her hands of learning anything about Islaam. Therefore it is required that you obtain a strong understanding of this religion of Allaah, and then spread it to the farthest degree of your ability from beneficial books.

I also advise those young women who adhere to the religion to give significant attention to marrying a man who also strives to adhere to the religion, as establishing and building a family that strives to hold fast to Islaam is something to be sought after. And the Messenger, may Allaah's praise and salutation be upon him and his family, said, *{The individual is upon the religion of his associate or friend}* [1]. And he also said, *{The example of the righteous companion and the evil companion is like the example of sitting with the musk seller and the blacksmith. So from the musk seller, either he will give you some as a gift, or you would buy some musk or at the least enjoy from him a good pleasing smell. But as for sitting with the blacksmith either your clothes with be burned, or at the least you will experience a bad nasty smell.}* [2], found

---

[1]    Narrated in Sunan Abu Daawud: 4833/ Jaame'a at-Tirmidhee: 2378/ & Musnad Imaam Ahmad: 7968, 8212/ -from the hadeeth of Abu Hurairah. It was declared authentic by Sheikh al-Albaanee in Silsilat al-Hadeeth as-Saheehah :927, Mishkaat al-Masaabeh: 5019, Saheeh al-Jaame'a as-Sagheer: 5858, his verification of al-'Emaan by Ibn Taymeeyah page 55, as well as in Saheeh Sunan Abu Dawud, & Saheeh Sunan at-Tirmidhee. Sheikh Muqbil declared it authentic in al-Jaame'a al-Saheeh: 4565, 4292.

[2]    Narrated in Saheeh al-Bukhaaree: 2101, 5534/ Saheeh Muslim: 2628/ -on the authority of Abu Moosa al-'Asha'ree. And it is in Sunan Abu Daawud: 4829/ -on the authority of 'Anas Ibn Maalik. It was declared authentic by Sheikh al-Albaanee in Silsilat al-Hadeeth as-Saheehah: 3214, Mishkaat al-Masaabeh: 5010, Saheeh at-Targheeb at-Tarheeb: 3064, 3065, Saheeh al-Jaame'a as-Sagheer: 2365, 5828, 5829, 5839, as well as in Saheeh Sunan Abu Dawud.

in both of two most authentic hadeeth collections, Saheeh al-Bukhaaree and Saheeh Muslim, as narrated by Abu Musaa. But do not be fooled, as the saying goes about meat, "Not everything that is white is truly a piece of delicious fat." So do not suppose that every individual who allows his beard to grow, and wears an imaamah as a turban, and makes his thawb so that it only comes to the middle of his shin is someone who is now a Sunni Muslim. As perhaps he may be from the astray sect of the Mukaramah who are worse in their evil than the Christians and the Jews. Perhaps he may be someone who only resembles the people of the Sunnah in the affairs of practicing his religion and other matters. As such it is required that a woman know the condition of a man before she is married to him. But as for the case where she would learn well and then become someone who is a caller to Allaah and His religion, and then she is thrown into a situation by her greedy father, who "sells" her in marriage for a hundred thousand Yemenee Riyals, he sells her just like one sells a product! No, rather it is obligatory that one look for a righteous man who is suitable, and then in addition that he gives from his wealth. So if one is tested with the like of this circumstance, then it is better for her to temporarily put to the side the matter of marriage until Allaah makes it easy for her to marry a righteous man.

*[FROM 'A DEFENDING MISSION FROM AUDIO LECTURES UPON THE PEOPLE OF IGNORANCE & SOPHISTRY': VOL. 1, PAGE 92]*

# (24)

QUESTION: WHAT IS THE WORK OF THE FEMALE CALLER TO ALLAAH, AS YOU STATE THAT THE MESSENGER OF ALLAAH, MAY ALLAAH'S PRAISE AND SALUTATIONS BE UPON HIM AND HIS FAMILY, SAID: "NARRATE FROM ME EVEN IF IT IS A SINGLE STATEMENT." AND YOU MENTIONS THE STATEMENT, "THE ONE WHO CONCEALS KNOWLEDGE, IT WILL BE A BRIDLE UPON HIM ON THE DAY OF JUDGMENT." SO IS IT UPON A WOMAN TO TEACH EVERY MATTER THAT YOU TEACH, OR IS IT ESTABLISHED THAT THIS IS NOT PERMITTED FOR HER?

nswer: Allaah the Most Glorified and the Most Exalted says, ❖*So keep your duty to Allaah and fear Him as much as you can.*❖-(Surah at-Taghaabun: 16). So I advise her to memorize *((Riyadh as-Saaliheen)02-11)* and from the book *((al-Lu'Lu wa' al-Marjaan feemaa Itifaq Aleeheh as-Sheikhayn)07-01)*, as well as from the different verses of the Qur'aan, and to engage in calling to Allaah among women even if that entails leaving some of her other work, especially if she sees that she has an effect upon the people. Indeed, the enemies of Islaam travel to the mountain tops and to wild and distant places just to call the Muslims towards apostasy from Islaam, or to Christianity, or towards some other way, path, or disbelieving ideology. Therefore it is suitable that we call and invite to Allaah, the Most Perfect and the Most High, and we strive hard and struggle in this. Still, it is not permissible that a woman stands up and gives a sermon among men, or is a teacher among men, as this is a societal trial, as has been previously mentioned. But she should teach her sisters, and young children whose ages reach seven or perhaps ten years old, who have not yet developed sexual desire towards women. But as for her standing among men and addressing them and inviting them then no, this is not something permissible. She can fulfill her obligation among and through women. As many Muslim women in different countries believe in supplicating to others than Allaah, thinking they may benefit them. This one supplicates to the one known as al-Khamsah. This one supplicates to 'Alee Ibn Abu Taalib. This one supplicates to al-Hasan. This one supplicates to al-Husayn. This one supplicates to this or that person from among Allaah's creation. In addition to this, there is the case where some Muslim women, if injustice is done to them, they look towards the sky and say, [I look towards Allaah and how spacious He is! ] Because she falsely believes that the sky and heavens are Allaah, the Most Perfect and the Most High. We generally are in great need, and you women are in great need, of striving hard and struggling in efforts of calling among women. In this there is tremendous good. And we seek Allaah's assistance in our affairs. Similar to this, is calling to Allaah by means of authoring and compiling works. It is proper that you delve into authoring works by taking from verses of the Qur'aan and authentic hadeeth narrations from the Prophet, may Allaah's praise and salutations be upon him and his family. As these other types of statements, meaning the speech and statement whose origin is from the people themselves, their intellectual meandering and philosophy, is not something which benefits and their popularity will not last.

Additionally, the woman must not call the people using a public microphone, and the voice of a woman may cause societal trials, as even now we hear on the radio the female announcers. May Allaah remove these female announcers from the Muslim radio programs. We fear for ourselves being put to trial, and so we disapprove of listening to these female announcers. So be those who simply invite women, as if you establish this obligation, then you all stand upon a tremendous good.

*[FROM 'A DEFENDING MISSION FROM AUDIO LECTURES UPON THE PEOPLE OF IGNORANCE & SOPHISTRY': VOL. 2, PAGE 478]*

# *(25)*

QUESTION: WHAT IS THE ISLAMIC RULING OF A WOMAN WHO FULFILLS ALL THE CONDITIONS OF SEEKING KNOWLEDGE WITHIN HER HOME, BUT DESPITE THIS GOES TO THE MASJID TO MEET HER SISTERS IN FAITH OR TO CONVEY TO THEM KNOWLEDGE THAT SHE HAS?

nswer: There is no harm in this, if she goes to the masjid and she believes that she is safe from falling into harm or trial, and safe from causing trials for men from outside of her family- then this is a good undertaking. Yet if the other women come to her in her own home then this is better and more of a safeguard for her. And in any case there is a tremendous obligation that is to be established by righteous women, and the responsibility upon them is a very significant burden indeed. Because it is in the area of the Muslim woman that tremendous corruption has entered into our Islamic societies, as the enemies of Islaam invite the Muslim woman towards the revealing and exposing of her beauty, as a tool being used to direct her and advance her towards other aims and objectives. Tremendous corruption has entered into our society in the area of women. The scholars of Somalia were not destroyed and burned except due to corruption that occurred related to women. Yet they have unnecessarily come out in Sana'a, in Riyadh, and in many other places- they have come out to participate in demonstrations which are something they have been pushed towards by those who are the enemies of Islaam. So I advise them strongly and severely, and we also ask Allaah to stop them from stop engaging in this practice, and that instead they engage in that which benefits Islaam and the Muslims.

*[FROM 'A DEFENDING MISSION FROM AUDIO LECTURES UPON THE PEOPLE OF IGNORANCE & SOPHISTRY': VOL. 2, PAGE 479]*

# (26)

QUESTION: IF A FEMALE SEEKER OF KNOWLEDGE STUDIES IN THE MASJID, SHE NEEDS TO REVIEW WHAT SHE HAS LEARNED WHILE AT THE MASJID WHEN SHE RETURNS HOME, AND THIS TAKES CONSIDERABLE TIME. HOWEVER, SHE UNDERSTANDS THAT NEEDED WORK IN HER HOME AWAITS HER, AS SHE NEEDS TO ASSIST HER MOTHER IN THE HOME. THE AFFAIRS OF HER HOME TAKE ALL OF HER TIME AND SEEKING KNOWLEDGE NEEDS FULL DEDICATION FROM HER. SO IF SHE IS OCCUPIED IN HER HOME, SHE IS NOT ABLE TO ACQUIRE A GREAT DEAL OF KNOWLEDGE. HOW CAN WE RECONCILE BETWEEN HER COMMITMENT TO HER HOME AND HER DEDICATION TO SEEKING KNOWLEDGE?

nswer: If she is able to avoid some of the worldly activities that she has to do, then I advise her to do so. If it is not possible to do that, then she should organize her time and give a significant part of it towards seeking knowledge, and then a part toward her worldly activities. It is not possible for anyone to acquire knowledge unless worldly matters are placed secondary to knowledge. As for the case where knowledge is made secondary in importance to the worldly matters, then it will not be acquired. And we ask Allaah to assist us.

*[FROM 'A DEFENDING MISSION FROM AUDIO LECTURES UPON THE PEOPLE OF IGNORANCE & SOPHISTRY': VOL. 2, PAGE 480]*

## (27)

QUESTION: A WOMAN STUDIES IN HER HOME AND PREFERS TO REMAIN IN HER HOME- NOT EVEN GOING OUT TO THE MASJID. IS SHE BETTER, OR THE WOMAN WHO SEEKS KNOWLEDGE OUTSIDE AND VISITS DIFFERENT MASJIDS?

nswer: The woman who stays within her home and learns within her home is better, because the Prophet, may Allaah's praise and salutation be upon him and his family, said: *{Do not prevent the maidservants of Allaah from attending the masjids, but their houses are better for them.}* [1].

*[FROM 'A DEFENDING MISSION FROM AUDIO LECTURES UPON THE PEOPLE OF IGNORANCE & SOPHISTRY': VOL. 2, PAGE 481]*

---

[1]   Narrated in Sunan Abu Daawud: 480/ & Musnad Imaam Ahmad: 5445, 5448/ -on the authority of 'Abdullah Ibn 'Umar. It was declared authentic by Sheikh al-Albaanee in Irwa' al-Ghaleel: 515, and Saheeh Sunan Abu Dawud.

# (28)

QUESTION: I AM A FEMALE STUDENT OF KNOWLEDGE. I HAVE BEEN PROPOSED TO BY CLOSE TO 25 YOUNG MEN AND I REFUSED ALL OF THEM DURING THE PAST EIGHT YEARS. THIS WAS BECAUSE I DID NOT FEEL COMFORTABLE WITH ANY DECISION AFTER MAKING SALAT AL-ISTIKHARAH TO ALLAAH THE MOST GLORIFIED AND THE MOST EXALTED. HOWEVER, MY FAMILY HAS BLAMED ME FREQUENTLY REGARDING THE FAILURE TO MARRY BY SAYING, "WHAT IS IMPORTANT IS ANY MAN WHO IS ACCEPTABLE." BUT I HAVE PROMISED MYSELF THAT I WOULD ONLY MARRY A BROTHER WHO ADHERES TO THE SUNNAH, AND STRIVES IN THE WAY OF ALLAAH WITH HIS WEALTH, WORDS AND HIS SELF. SO IS THIS PERMISSIBLE?

nswer: This is permissible, if Allaah so wills, as the righteous companion assists you in doing good, as has been previously mentioned. A woman might be righteous and then marry a man who is a wrongdoer. In a very short time he will distract, distance, and busy her away from that previous good she was established upon. Rather, what I advise is choosing for marriage a righteous man, even if it requires spending of her own wealth for this, if she possesses it, or providing their housing even she didn't have wealth. So in light of this, she shouldn't intentionally choose a life of remaining unmarried, as, all praise is due to Allaah, the righteous people are many in Algeria and in other lands. Indeed there are those from among righteous people who are wishing and looking for righteous women. How excellent it would be if you were to marry a righteous man and establish a righteous Muslim family, establishing the call of inviting to the Book of Allaah and the Sunnah of the Messenger of Allaah, may Allaah's praise and salutations be upon him and his household. Therefore, all praise is due to Allaah, the righteous men are numerous.

I know of some brothers from Algeria, and all praise is due to Allaah, they are righteous men. Even from the students of knowledge who are here with us there are righteous men who are upright on Allaah's path from our students from Algeria, may Allaah preserve them, and they wish for and are seeking righteous women to marry, even to the degree that they might remain here in Yemen after marriage with her. Yet if Allaah so wills, they will travel to call to Allaah to places such as America and many other lands.

Regarding choosing a righteous woman for marriage, it is narrated in the two 'Saheeh' Collections of Imaam al-Bukhaaree and Imaam Muslim and the authority of 'Aishah, may Allaah be pleased with her, that the Prophet, may Allaah's praise and salutations be upon him and his household, said:

*{A woman is married for four things: her wealth, her family status, her beauty and her religion. So you should marry the religious woman otherwise you will be from the losers.}*- (Saheeh al-Bukhaaree: 5090, Saheeh Muslim: 1466). So a man should choose a righteous woman and a woman should chose a righteous man. Otherwise, if this is not the case then the situation will be as found in the statement of the Messenger of Allaah, may Allaah's praise and salutations be upon him and his household, *{A person is upon the religion of his close associate so look closely at who you take as a close friend.}* [1]. We do not make it a condition that the person be free of any mistakes or does not commit any sins, as perhaps such a person does not exist. But indeed how excellent is the statement of the one who said,

> As for the one who possesses that overall character and nature that you are pleased with,
>
>> Then content yourself with this noble one, and look beyond his minor shortcomings.

And another person said:

> I am not one who runs after the faults of my brother or gathers his faults,
>
>> As at the times which he is untidy and disordered, what man could be considered well mannered and cultured!

So it is required to overlook some matters. I am not saying that a woman should marry a man who is a wrongdoer, or marry the one whose heart is committed to seeking worldly wealth; but if a student of knowledge comes who loves knowledge then this is the one to choose. He might be one

[1]    Narrated in Sunan Abu Dawud: 4833/ Jaame'a at-Tirmidhee: 2378/ Musnad Imaam Ahmad: 7978, 8212/ -on the authority of Abu Hurairah. It was declared authentic by Sheikh al-Albaanee in Silsilat al-Hadeeth as-Saheehah: 927, Mishkaat al-Masaabeh: 5019, & Saheeh al-Jaame'a as-Sagheer: 5858, and in his verification of al-'Emaan by Ibn Taymeeyah. Sheikh Muqbil declared it authentic in al-Jaame'a al-Saheeh: 4265, 4292.

who has memorized the Qur'aan, or a caller, or one who writes that which invites to Allaah and His religion, and through such a righteous woman is blessed in this to be able to call to Allaah, the Most Perfect and the Most High. Such a situation should be considered the Paradise of this world. And we seek Allaah's assistance in our affairs.

*[FROM 'A DEFENDING MISSION FROM AUDIO LECTURES UPON THE PEOPLE OF IGNORANCE & SOPHISTRY': VOL. 2, PAGE 486]*

# (29)

QUESTION: WHAT IS THE ISLAMIC RULING REGARDING ORGANIZING OUR ISLAMIC EFFORTS IN REGARD TO WOMEN, WITH THOSE EFFORTS BEING IN THE MASJID? THAT BEING, FOR EXAMPLE, A SISTER WHO TAKES THE RESPONSIBILITY OF STRAIGHTENING THE ROWS OF THE WOMEN, AND A SISTER WHO TAKES THE RESPONSIBILITY OF MAKING SURE THE MENSTRUATING WOMEN ARE SEPARATED IN A DIFFERENT AREA, AND A SISTER WHO TAKES THE RESPONSIBILITY FOR THE MANAGEMENT OF A LIBRARY BY USING CARDS FOR ITS ADMINISTRATION. THESE YOUNG WOMEN WOULD REMAIN LATER AFTER THE OTHER WOMEN HAVE LEFT IN ORDER TO AVOID ANY DISORGANIZATION.

nswer: This is something good and there is no harm in it, insh'Allaah, as Islaam encourages organization which is not related to any innovation in the religion. Such library cards should be made without the images of living things, as the Messenger of Allaah may Allaah's praise and salutation be upon him and his family, said, *{The angels do not enter a house within which there are images or a dog.}*-(Saheeh al-Bukhaaree: 3225, 3322, 4002/ Saheeh Muslim: 2106)

*[FROM A DEFENDING MISSION FROM AUDIO LECTURES UPON THE PEOPLE OF IGNORANCE & SOPHISTRY': VOL. 2, PAGE 479]*

# (30)

QUESTION: WE SEE THAT SOME PEOPLE DO NOT GIVE IMPORTANCE TO SEEKING KNOWLEDGE FROM THE HANDS OF THE SCHOLARS AND ARE SATISFIED WITH STUDYING BOOKS IN THEIR HOMES. THEY ARGUE THAT SHEIKH AL-ALBAANEE (MAY ALLAAH THE EXALTED PRESERVE HIM) WAS ABLE TO REACH THE LEVEL OF KNOWLEDGE THAT HE POSSESSES SOLELY BY MEANS OF READING, NOT BY MEANS OF TAKING FROM THE SCHOLARS THEMSELVES. IS THIS CORRECT AND WITH WHAT DO YOU ADVISE THE ONE WHO SAYS THIS?

nswer: That which I advise him is that if he is able to, then he should attend the gatherings of the scholars, because at times sitting with a scholar can be equal in its benefit to reading for an entire month. Yet if it is not possible for one to sit with the scholars, then he should have a library for his study and should correspond with the people of knowledge, consulting and seeking clarifications from them and striving in a good way. But how would this be implemented? If he has a book and he is sure that it is from so-and-so who is trustworthy then there is no harm in reading it and benefiting from it. As for the different meaning of statements and expressions of the scholars then these will eventually become clear in the mind of the individual reading them. I still recall some of the statements of my Sheikh, Muhammad Ibn 'Abdul-Wahaab as-Somaalee, may Allaah the Exalted preserve him, from his lessons in the sanctuary of Masjid al-Haram in Mecca.

However, if there are no scholars available or he is not able to attend, then he should have a library, and rely upon Allaah, the Most Perfect and the Most High to successfully learn. But be warned with a serious warning of the slips, unintentionally misleading statements, and those statements that conflict with what is correct that come from the established, well-known scholars that he may read. As such it is upon him to submit and compare his own thinking and ideas to that to the thinking and ideas held by the early scholars of this Ummah. And I am not inviting one to simply blindly follow them, as blind following is generally impermissible in the religion. Rather, he must seek to be guided by their understanding. Then in proceeding in this way a library is something good and is a blessing from Allaah, the Most Perfect and the Most High, and it makes the use of books easier. Perhaps this present availability of books were never this easy for many of the early Muslim scholars. If one of us was charged with having to copy *((Fath al-Baaree)03-01)* by hand, as perhaps they did, he would not be able to do so!

*[ FROM 'A DEFENDING MISSION FROM AUDIO LECTURES UPON THE PEOPLE OF IGNORANCE & SOPHISTRY': VOL. 1, PAGE 63]*

# (31)

QUESTION: WHAT ARE THE BOOKS RELATED THE SUBJECT OF UNDERSTANDING HOW TO CORRECTLY PRACTICE THE RELIGION THAT YOU ADVISE ME AND THOSE WHO ARE WITH ME TO READ?

nswer: The book which we advise you with is ((al-Muhalla)08-07) from Abee Muhammad Ibn Hazm, may Allaah have mercy upon him, while putting aside and staying away from his severity and harshness with regard to those who differed with him, as well as his stubborn adherence to the 'Dhareeyah' school of fiqh. Likewise this also applies to the mistakes of Abee Muhammad (Ibn Hazm) in the matters of belief. After this work, then ((Nayl al-Awtar)03-08) of Shawkanee, then ((al-Majmu'a)08-04) of Nawawee, then ((al-Mughnee)07-07) of Ibn Qudamah. Along with what will come of your many questions, you should not refer to the books of compiled rulings except when you have a definite need. I also say to you, I do not refer to such books of compiled rulings except when I have a clear need related to an issue that has come forward which requires this. Were we to spend so much of our time in such books, then we would not be able to gain beneficial knowledge in other branches of knowledge. There might be six, ten, or even twenty different opinions or positions regarding a specific issue. Due to this we advise a comprehensive commitment to referring first and foremost to the Book and the Sunnah, and then to acquiring the books of fiqh and benefiting from them in the situations in which you have a need.

*[FROM 'A DEFENDING MISSION FROM AUDIO LECTURES UPON THE PEOPLE OF IGNORANCE & SOPHISTRY': VOL. 1, PAGE 275]*

# (32)

# BOOKS OF GUIDANCE & BOOKS OF MISGUIDANCE.[1]

---

[1]    This extraordinary selection was the original heart of this compilation as well as the original map that was used to build the library of books for our household, and any success is from Allaah. An additional note to the reader is that the specifics related to the availability and preference of certain printings was specific to the original time of presentation and in many cases these have now changed quite significantly, as the availability of beneficial books has increased tremendously- alhamdulillah. Please refer to our website for current book information connected to the recommended book list which we hope to continually update insh'allaah.

All praise is due to Allaah Lord of all the worlds, may Allaah's praise and salutations be upon our Prophet, his household, and all his Companions. I bear witness there is none worthy of worship other than Allaah alone, having no partner. And I bear witness that Muhammad is his worshipper and Messenger. As for what follows: Indeed the Imaams al-Bukhaaree and Muslim have narrated within their two 'Saheeh' collections, on the authority of Mu'aweeyah, may Allaah, the Most High be pleased with him, that the Prophet, may Allaah's praise and salutations be upon him and his household, said, *{Whoever Allaah intends good for He grants him understanding in the religion.}* [2]. And it is narrated in their two 'Saheeh' collections on the authority of Abu Musaa al-'Asha'ree, may Allaah, the Most High be pleased with him, that the Prophet, may Allaah's praise and salutations be upon him and his household, said, *{ The example of guidance and knowledge with which Allaah has sent me is like abundant rain falling on the earth, some of which was fertile soil that absorbed rain water and brought forth vegetation and grass in abundance. Another portion of it was hard and held the rain water and Allaah benefited the people with it and they utilized it for drinking, letting their animals drink from it and for irrigation of the land for cultivation. A portion of it was barren, and could neither hold the water nor bring forth vegetation (so that land gave no benefits). The first is the example of the person who comprehends Allah's religion and gets benefit from the knowledge and guidance which Allah has revealed through me  and learns and then teaches others. The last example is that of a person who does not care for it*

[2]    Narrated in Saheeh al-Bukhaaree: 71, 3116, 7312/ Saheeh Muslim: 1037/ Sunan Ibn Maajah: 221/ al-Muwatta Maalik: 1300, 1667/Musnad Imaam Ahmad: 16395: 16404, and other than these two/ Musannaf Ibn Abee Shaybah:31792/ Sunan ad-Daaramee: 224, 226/- on the authority of Mu'aweeyah, and  it is found in Jaame'a al-Tirmidhee: 2645/ Musnad Imaam Ahmad: 2786 /Sunan ad-Daaramee: 270, 2706/- on the authority of Ibn 'Abbaas, and  it is found in Sunan Ibn Maajah:220/ Musannaf 'Abdul-Razzaaq: 30851/- on the authority of Abu Hurairah. It was declared authentic by Sheikh al-Albaanee in Saheeh al-Aadab al-Mufrad: 517, Silsilat al-Hadeeth as-Saheehah: 1194, 1195, 1196, Saheeh at-Targheeb at-Tarheeb: 67, as well as in other of his books. Sheikh Muqbil declared it authentic in al-Jaame'a al-Saheeh: 9, 3123, 4650, may Allaah have mercy upon them both.

*and does not accept Allaah's guidance revealed through me. (He is like that barren land.)}* -(Saheeh al-Bukhaaree: 79, & Saheeh Muslim: 2282). Muslim narrated in his 'Saheeh' collection on the authority of Abu Hurairah, may Allaah be pleased with him, that the Prophet, upon him and his family be Allaah's praises and the best of salutations, said:, *{When a son of Aadam dies his deeds end except for three matters: a continuing charity, a righteous child who supplicates for him, or knowledge by which others are benefited.}* [3].

Therefore when we read from and listen to *((Saheeh al-Bukhaaree)02-01)* or *((Saheeh Muslim)02-02)* or *((Tafseer Ibn Katheer)01-01)* or *((Musnad of Imaam Ahmad)02-07)* or other works which are from the books of the Sunnah, then that author is rewarded for this, by the permission of Allaah the Most High, according to the evidence which we have just heard- that one's works cease after his death except for three. And from them is knowledge by which others are benefited.

A book is to be considered a sitting companion, so it is only proper that you select a righteous companion. al-Bukhaaree and Muslim have narrated in their two 'Saheeh' collections, on the authority of Abu Musaa al-'Asha'ree, may Allaah be pleased with him, that the Prophet, may Allaah's praise and salutations be upon him and his household, said, *{The example of the righteous companion and the evil companion is like the example of sitting with the musk seller and the blacksmith. So from the musk seller, either he will give you some as a gift, or you would buy some musk or at the least enjoy from him a good pleasing smell. But as for sitting with the blacksmith either your clothes with be burned, or at the least you will experience a bad nasty smell.}* [4].

---

[3]    Narrated in Saheeh Muslim: 1631/ Sunan Abu Dawud: 2880/ Jaame'a at-Tirmidhee: 1376/  Sunan an-Nasaa'ee: 3681/ Musnad Imaam Ahmad: 8627/ & Sunan ad-Daaramee: 559/-on the authority of Abu Hurairah. It was declared authentic by Sheikh al-Albaanee in Saheeh at-Targheeb at-Tarheeb: 78, 93, Mishkaat al-Masaabeeh: 127, 203, & Saheeh al-Jaame'a as-Sagheer: 793, and the three 'Sunan' collections.
[4]    Narrated in Saheeh al-Bukhaaree: 2101, 5534/ Saheeh Muslim: 2628/ -on the authority of Abu Moosa al-'Asha'ree. And it is in Sunan Abu Daawud: 4829/ -on the

In these days we often find there are book fairs, and the righteous people use and busy themselves at them for good, while the people of wrongdoing use and busy themselves at them for evil and wrongdoing. During one of the previous years there was found at one of the fairs a book entitled [[The Neighing Form]] which contained outright disbelief in Islaam, and cast false accusations against the Prophet Yusuf. Accusations that I am not even able to speak about, even worse accusations than adultery! Indeed a significant door of evil is opened by books of deviation and misguidance. But as for true books of goodness, then it is falsely said by some [The Wahaabee Books are dangerous!] They have no shame in expressing their ignorance such that they say,[Saheeh al-Bukhaaree is a Wahaabee book!] Oh you poor ignorant one, Imaam al-Bukhaaree is from the scholars of the third century, but as for Muhammad Ibn 'Abdul-Wahaab it has only been one hundred and fifty or two hundred years ago, or something similar to this, since he died, may Allaah have mercy upon him! So how many centuries are there between Imaam al-Bukhaaree and between Muhammad Ibn 'Abdul-Wahaab?!? And perhaps al-Bukhaaree's book might be that which delivers and saves you from entering Hellfire. How excellent is the speech of the poet who said:

*She said, "Oh you, you have spent upon books until your hands empty."*

*Yet I replied, "Leave me alone,*

*As perhaps I may find among them a book that will guide me,*

*So that tomorrow I will be able to take my book of deeds with my right hand*

---

authority of 'Anas Ibn Maalik. It was declared authentic by Sheikh al-Albaanee in Silsilat al-Hadeeth as-Saheehah: 3214, Mishkaat al-Masaabeeh: 5010, Saheeh at-Targheeb at-Tarheeb: 3064, 3065, Saheeh al-Jaame'a as-Sagheer: 2365, 5828, 5829, 5839, as well as in Saheeh Sunan Abu Dawud.

And it has been said, "*The clever one in a matter is devoted to knowledge and dedicated to writings*". And it has been said,

*If we are the companions of rulers and kings they act arrogantly with us,*

> *They belittle and undervalue the right of the sitting companion.*

*And if we sit as companions of the business men and traders we lean towards worldly matters,*

> *becoming those concerned with counting money.*

*So we stick to our houses, and extract knowledge*

> *and fill the blank pages of books with it.*

This was the case of our scholars from the first generations whose works benefited the Muslims and the non-Muslims. They wrote, may Allaah have mercy upon them, many volumes. Often they will compose an entire volume regarding a single issue, such as the question about when reciting as the imaam in certain prayers, should the verse "*Bismillah ar-Rahman ar-Raheem*" be recited aloud or recited quietly. And I am not trying to say that you will find one book on these issues, rather there are many scholars who individually wrote entire volumes discussing a single issue! For example Ibn Jawzee, Khateeb al-Baghdadee, ad-Darqutnee, and Ibn 'Abdul-Bar - each have written a work about this entitled, *((Insaaf fee Masi'alat ul-Khilaaf)07-24)*. These four scholars all wrote works about this single issue of how to recite the basmallah. What is correct in this issue is that it should be recited quietly. This is what is correct due to what is narrated by the scholars al-Bukhaaree and Muslim in their two 'Saheeh' collections, on the authority of 'Anas, may Allaah be pleased with him, where he said, *{I prayed behind the Messenger of Allaah, may Allaah's praise and salutations be upon him and his household, Abu Bakr, and 'Umar, and they all began their audible recitation with the verse "Alhamdulillahi* *rabbil 'Alaameen."}* Therefore this is what is soundest from among the various statements of the people of knowledge. But it is not this specific issue which I intended as my point, this was only put forward as an example.

The people differ in relation to the issue of benefiting from books, so it is proper for the common person to acquire the following books: *((Riyaadh as-Saaliheen)02-11)*, *((Tafseer Ibn Katheer)01-01)*, *((Bulugh al-Maraam)02-34)*, *((Fath al-Majeed Sharh Kitaab at-Tawheed)06-12)*, *((Ad-Dur an-Nadheed Fee Ikhlaas Kalamaat at-Tawheed)06-11)*, and this is the last work by ash-Shawkaanee, *((Tat-heer al-'Itiqaad 'An Adraan al-'Ilhaad)06-30)* by Sana'anee. These books are what it is proper that the general Muslim acquire, as well as *((Lu'Lu' wa al-Marjaan Feemaa 'Itifaaq 'Aleihi as-Sheikhaan)02-16)*.

As for the individual who is at a higher level of knowledge than the general Muslim, then it is proper that he acquire the following books:

*((Saheeh al-Bukhaaree)02-01)*

*((Saheeh Muslim)02-02)*

And similarly if you are able to acquire the remaining four hadeeth collections which are all together known as the "*Six Mother Collections of Hadeeth*" then this is good. These works are for the like of someone who is literate and reads and writes well; someone who simply loves knowledge. These books are, all praise is due to Allaah, easy to read works. As for the one who is a researcher, then it is proper for him to be diligent in trying to acquire all of the books of the Sunnah. It is not suitable that he neglect a single book from the acknowledged books of the Sunnah if he has the ability to get it. This is in view of the fact that our scholars, may Allaah grant them and us the success of attaining every good, are often occupied with their strictly scheduled work of livelihood and employment, such that their working hours are in the morning, after dhuhr, and they have a gathering between maghrib and 'ishaa' or after salatul 'ishaa'. One of them may be a judge, so that after his working hours it is necessary that he take with him cases that he must rule upon, so that he can read and review them after hours. This busy schedule is enough to make one go crazy, especially as the scholar does not have any time available to sit with his students or to review that which he has learned.

So considering that our scholars are often busy with their positions and employments and have left teaching, then it is only proper and necessary for the student of knowledge to be diligent and have significant concern for acquiring good books, which will repel from him misguidance and straying from the straight path. From the students of knowledge are those who have graduated from the Islamic University in Medinahh Munawarrah or from al-Azhaar University in Egypt, or from the Main University in Sana'a, or from al-Haadee University in Sa'ada, or other than these universities. But before you know it they have become one who chooses something over the reward found with Allaah, and so become as is said:

> Concerned with gaining knowledge in every land are youth,
>
>> but when they have achieved it and gathered it,
>
> Then after having mastered the chains of the transmission and its principles,
>
>> and having become scholars, they then waste it and turn their backs on it.
>
> They lean towards worldly gains, milking them,
>
>> going against their knowledge, and ignoring it.
>
> So oh evil scholars where are your intellects and where now are,
>
>> your connected hadeeth narrations of the chosen prophet!

And, all praise is due to Allaah, the books are available and present, may Allaah reward our scholars with good. We advise the students of knowledge to be diligent in acquiring books, even to the degree that he sells his car or his turban in order to purchase a book of guidance. Indeed, a single book of guidance may be equal to the contents of the entire world. For the student who is also a researcher it is also possible that he acquires the main well known hadeeth collections by means of buying their explanations such as:

*((Fath al-Baaree Sharh Saheeh al-Bukhaaree)03-01)*, and the best printing of this is the 'Salafeeyah' edition due to what it incorporated indicating the different location of hadeeth narrations.

*((Saheeh Muslim be Sharh an-Nawawee)03-02)*

*((Sunan Abu Dawud Ma' 'Awn al-Ma'bood)03-03)* this is printed in two different editions, one from Egypt and the other from India.

*((Tuhfat al-Awadha Sharh Jaame'a at-Tirmidhee)03-04)*; likewise, this is printed in two different editions, one from Egypt and the other from India. The Indian edition is most correct and is five volumes along with an introduction. But the Egyptian printing is printed such that it is easier for the student of knowledge to read.

*((Sunan Ibn Majaah)03-05)* with a concise and excellent commentary. It has now been printed with the verification of Muhammad Fouad 'Abdul-Baaqee

*((Sunan an-Nasaa'ee)02-03)* This is the smaller Sunan compiled by Nasaa'ee which has marginal notes by Sindee and Suyootee. It has been numbered and indexed by Abu Ghuddah.

*((Musnad of Imaam Ahmad)02-07)*; if you are able to acquire the verification of this work by Ahmad Shaakir then do so. Otherwise the Musnad of Ahmad in six large volumes, and searching within it is difficult. But Allaah facilitates research in it thorough utilizing an index compiled for this printing.

*((Musannaf 'Abdur-Razzaq)02-15)*

*((Musannaf Ibn Abee Shaybah)02-14)*

*((Musnad Abee Ya'laa)02-18)*

*((Kashf al-Astaar 'An Zawa'id al-Zubaar)02-17)*

*((Musnad al-Humaydee)02-19)*

*((Saheeh Ibn Hibaan)02-13)* which is favored by some of the scholars

*((Saheeh Ibn Khuzaymah)02-20)*

The three Mu'jam collections by at-Tabaree: *((Mu'jam al-Kabeer)02-21)*, *((al-Awsaat)02-22)*, and *((as-Sagheer)02-23)*. Additionally, there are other beneficial books which it is proper to acquire, such as:

*((Talkhees al-Khabeer)04-03)* by Haafidh Ibn Hajr

*((Nasab ar-Raawee fee Takhreej Ahadeeth al-Hadaaeyah)04-05)* by Zayla'ee

*((Nayl al-Awtaar)03-08)* by Shawkaanee

*((Subl as-Salaam)03-06)* by as-Sana'anee. Also, all the books of Sheikh Naasirudden al-Albaanee should be acquired, as a researcher cannot do without the books of Sheikh Naasirudden al-Albaanee, may Allaah the Exalted preserve him. And from the important books of fiqh, or understanding how to correctly apply the guidance of the source texts, are:

*((al-Muhalaa)08-07)* by Abu Muhammad Ibn Hazm

*((al-Ahkaam fee Usul al-Ahkaam)08-02)* by Abu Muhammad Ibn Hazm

*((Zaad al-Ma'ad Fee Haadee Khair al-Ebaad)09-05)*

*((al-Mughnee)07-07)* by Ibn Qudaamah

*((Tarh at-Tathreeb fee Sharh Taqreeb al-Asaaneed)04-06)* by Haafidh al-Iraaqee and his son.

*((Majma' az-Zawa'id)02-24)*

*((al-Mutaalib al-'Aleeyah)12-32)*

*((al-Mustradraak)02-25)*

*((al-Hilyaah)05-03)*

As for the one who enjoys reading and has a love of knowledge, I don't believe it is possible for him not to have a library. As perhaps he will be reading and come across a hadeeth and its source is another book. So he says, "*This is a book that I must purchase.*" Myself, when I was compiling the work *((at-Talea'ah Fee Rad 'Alaa Ghulaat as-Shee'ah)11-12)*, at that time I had a large bookcase and I used to suppose that I had gathered the books of the world within it. But when I began writing this book, I came to references to other source works which I did not possess. So then I was diligent in acquiring those specific source books I lacked. Then afterwards when I was compiling *((as-Saheeh al-Musnad Min Asbaab an-Nuzul)01-10)* I again came to realize that my library was still deficient. But it was Allaah, the Most Perfect and the Most High, was the One Who made it easy for me to raise the money for those books even if I had to borrow some of it. At one time I had wanted to buy the book *((Tadheeb at-Tadheeb)05-18)* by Haafidh Ibn Hajr, and it was around 200 Saudi Riyaals. I was living in Mecca and said to one of my companions, "*Loan me some money.*" He said, "*For what?*" I replied "*There is a book that I wish to buy.*" He said, "*No. If you have a need in relation to something for your household or family, or clothing, or something like this, then I will lend you money. But I will not lend it to you for a book.*" However, before he knew it, somehow I had purchased the book. Later he asked me, "*Where did you get the money from?*" I said, "*Allaah, the Most Perfect and the Most High made it easy for me.*" And this was our brother from the sake of Allaah, who we loved for the sake of Allaah. May Allaah reward him with good. So if a person gives importance to acquiring books, then Allaah, the Most Perfect and the Most High makes this easy. I do not mean that you should gather books just for appearance as some of the people do. We visit some of the people from Ahlus-Sunnah and find that they have a brand new library, yet his state is as is said:

*There are a large number of volumes with the Sheikh,*

*but in truth, he does not actually read them.*

Rather, acquire books and then devote yourself to reading them. Just as the wife of Imaam az-Zuhree said to him when she found him so engrossed with his books, and perhaps lacking in the time spent interacting with her. She said, *"By Allaah, your books are harder on me than if you had three more wives!"* In such a way this is necessary for the student of knowledge, if he makes the goal of gaining beneficial knowledge secondary to pursuing worldly aims then he will not gain significant knowledge. The same is the case if he makes knowledge merely a means to attain worldly benefits, or makes his efforts of calling to Allaah and His religion a means to worldly benefit

And we must go back to examine the books of criticism and commendation in the religion. These books are indeed important, and Allaah has given our scholars success. When you read the biographies contained within these books, you are always coming across important points of knowledge. This is if you read works such as *((Mizaan al-'Itidaal)05-19)*. As *((Mizaan al-'Itidaal)05-19)* has been said to be the best book written by Imaam adh-Dhahabee, such that some of the Hanafees, the Asha'rees, and the Shee'ah feel tormented by this work! They say, [If adh-Dhahabee writes the biography of a Hanafee scholar or an Asha'ree then he shortens his biography, but when it is the biography of a Hanbalee scholar he lengthens it extensively!!] But ash-Shawkaanee staes in *((al-Badr al-Talaa')05-29)*: *"No this is not correct. However this man, Imaam adh-Dhahabee, was a man whose heart drank deeply from the knowledge of hadeeth, such that if he writes the biography of a scholar of hadeeth he gives free rein to his pen in composing such a biography; but when he is composing the biography of someone who is not a scholar of hadeeth then he does not have the same concern."* As for the Shee'ah, then he protected *((Mizaan)05-19)* from being filled with their madness. To the degree that they said:

*In the scale the book al-Mizaan mostly inclines towards*

*the like of those mentioned in Surah ar-Rahmaan*

*So (oh Shee'ah people) openly declare the deficiency of the one*

*who denies the rightful place of the prophet's family,*

*While you raise their level and position, such that you break the thorn*

*which is the book al-Mizaan.*

But all praise is due to Allaah, in fact it is *((al-Mizaan)05-19)* which actually throws a tremendous blow and breaks them, while they have not struck any blow against it. The people have not ceased competing with each other to acquire *((Mizaan al-'Itidaal)05-19)* and *((Lisaan al-Mizaan)05-20)*, and other books by Imaam adh-Dhahabee may Allaah, the Most High, have mercy upon him. Additional beneficial books for the researcher are: *((Taarikh Baghdaad)09-03)* and *((Taarikh Ibn 'Asaakir)09-10)*, the copies of which the people of Sa'adah stole from me when the shipment reached there from al-Qaseem, Saudi Arabia. They consider it war booty in their conflict with us as Ahlus-Sunnah, so they always stall their release in hopes that we will simply leave the books to them in frustration. The individual who stole them is the one who is responsible for the various media and news in Sa'adah.

And this book is one you cannot do without, and is from those beneficial books about which it is said, "*If an individual is to acquire of the books of biography and information about men, he must acquire ((at-Taarikh al-Kabeer)05-21) by al-Bukhaaree.*" It is a book of history, biography, commendation and criticism of men, indicating the hidden defects of narrations, as well as declaring narrations authentic or weak. It is a valuable book which it is proper that you acquire. And the book *((Jarh wa at-Ta'deel)04-07)* by Ibn Abe Haatim, as perhaps there is a narrator which is mentioned in *((at-Taarikh)05-21)* of al-Bukhaaree without any commendation or criticism, but you will find that he has been mentioned and spoken about within *((Jarh wa at-Ta'deel)04-07)* by Ibn Abe Haatim. As for *((Taarikh Baghdaad)09-03)* then certainly it has been said about it that it is proper that it be named "*History of the World.*" This is because in its age and time it was the capital of the Muslim world, and scholars come to it from every single Muslim country of the earth. Therefore it is considered a biography of the majority of the Muslim scholars of that time. Also from the beneficial books in history are the *((History of Ibn Ma'een)09-06)* may Allaah the Most High have mercy upon him, and that of *((ad-Darqutnee)09-07)*, may Allaah the Most High have mercy upon him. Similarly, there are the books of biography from the Companions such as: *((al-'Isaabah)05-02)*, and this is a tremendous book! But as for the book [[Hayat as-Sahabah]] it contains what is authentic as well as that which is false or inaccurate, so it is not suitable that it be held as reliable.

Similarly the book *((Asad al-Ghaabah)05-01)* is from the valuable books, as is the book *((al-'Isteea'aab)05-05)* by Haafidh Ibn 'Abdul-Bar. Additionally from the beneficial general reference works which it is proper that the student of knowledge acquire are the books of Sheikh al-Islaam Ibn Taymeeyah and Haafidh Ibn Qayyim, may Allaah have mercy upon them both. Indeed there is no opportunity to list their numerous books right now, as if they were all listed that itself would be enough to fill several pages of a book itself!

From the books that we haven't mentioned yet is *((as-Sunan al-Kubraa)02-31)* by al-Bayhaqee. It is an excellent book regarding issues of ritual worship and general rulings to the degree that some scholars have even said, "If there was any book that I was not able to do without, I would not be able to do without *((as-Sunan al-Kubraa)02-31)* of al-Bayhaqee regarding the matters of worship and rulings, rather than other books." There is also *((Ta'dheem Qadr as-Salaat)12-47)* by Muhammad Ibn Nasr al-Maruzee and *((al-Muntaqaa)12-21)* by Ibn Jaarood *((al-Musnad)02-32)* which is attributed to Imaam as-Shaafa'ee, and *((al-Bidaayah wa an-Nihaayah)09-02)* in the subject of History *((at-Tamheed)07-29)* by Ibn 'Abdul-Bar. Then there are the explanations of the Qur'aan from the first generations of Muslims *((Tafseer Haafidh Ibn Katheer)01-01)* and *((Tafseer Ibn Jareer)01-04)*, and *((Tafseer al-Baghawee)01-07)*. It is proper that you are diligent in striving to acquire these books of commentary, not simply relying upon the available summarized versions of *((Tafseer Ibn Katheer)01-01)*. Also it is proper that you acquire *((Tafseer Ibn Katheer)01-01)* itself, as it is from the most significant of references in explanation of the Qur'aan. It often transmits from books which we no longer have as existing manuscripts or printed copies in our time, and we find that it is transmitted with the reports with the chain of narration, whether authentic or weak. So it is a valuable work that is only proper you strive to have.

As for the books of correct beliefs from those known as the fundamental and best of works in this area are: *((as-Sunnah)02-26)*by Ibn Abee 'Aasim which Sheikh Naasirudden al-Albaanee, may Allaah the Most High preserve him, verified its narrations and investigated their sources and chains. And from them is *((as-Sunnah)06-22)* by 'Abdullah Ibn Ahmad Ibn Hanbal. And from them is the book *((al-'Asmaa' wa al-Sifaat)06-35)* by al-Bayhaqee, and *((Kitaab at-Taheed)06-36)* by Ibn Khuzaymah. The book *((al-'Emaan)06-37)* by Ibn Munduh. Also the book *((Tahaweeyah)06-08)*, yet if you are able to study the works of the earlier scholars, then this is easier on you, as *((Tahaweeyah)06-08)* has within it the false statements of the sect of the Kilaabeeyah, the Bishreeyah, the Mariseeyah, and others who were misguided- so this might be difficult upon you. But the works of the early scholars are not tarnished by the statements of the people of false philosophical rhetoric and so are easier to understand.

From those books which are precious is *((Kitaab as-Sharee'ah)06-34)* by al-Aajooree and the book *((ar-Rad 'Alaa al-Jahmeeyah)11-11)*, and *((Khalq 'Afaa'al al-'Ebaad)06-33)* as well as the book *((Sharh Usul 'Itiqaad Ahlus-Sunnah)06-29)* by Laalikkaa'ee. Now we move onto the those books related to the specific terminology of the sciences of hadeeth. Perhaps it is possible to limit this to the book *((al-Ba'ith al-Hatheeth)04-37)* if there is no one available to teach you. And possibly *((Tadreeb ar-Raawee)04-08)* and I mention these two works as both of them are easy and simple. But as for the case where you find someone to teach you, then *((Muqadamah Ibn Salaah)04-38)* and *((an-Nukat)04-04)* by Haafidh Ibn Hajr, *((at-Taqyeed wa al-Islaah)04-09)* by Haafidh al-'Iraaqee, *((al-Kifaayah)04-10)* by Haafidh al-Khateeb *((al-Jaame'a Li Akhlaaq ar-Raawee wa as-Saame'a)04-11)* by Haafidh al-Khateeb, and the book of ar-Raamhazmuzee which is considered the first book of this kind written on the subject of hadeeth science terminology and is named *((al-Muhadeeth al-Faasel)04-12)*. Also the book *((Fath al-Mugheeth)04-26)* despite its printing mistakes. I have been informed that others are working on a verification of this book, may Allaah assist them in this endeavor. Also there is *((Ma'rifat Uloom al-Hadeeth)04-13)* by Haakim, it is from the best of books. And the book *((Sharf Ashaabul Hadeeth)06-32)* is also from the best of books in this area. Likewise *((at-Tankeel Bemaa fee Ta'neeb al-Kawtharee Min Abaateel)04-27)* is also from the most excellent of books.

Now we will go to the books of the Arabic language. From them are those works which one may benefit from even without sitting with the scholars and learning from the people of knowledge, such as: *((al-Qaamoos)10-01)*, *((Taaj al-'Aroos)10-02)*, and *((Lisaan al-'Arab)10-03)*. They only speak about the meaning of individual words and terms. However, regarding the matter of learning grammar, then it is required the you seek its knowledge from the people of knowledge, because you may read something but not understand it. The area of usul al-fiqh, or the principles of jurisprudence, is similar; it is required that one benefit while learning it through some of the people of knowledge, as one may read something but not comprehend its full or correct meaning. Among the people there are those who gain understanding from significant reading and going over the various principles and guidelines found in works such as *((Nayl al-Awtaar)03-08)*, as you read over its discussion of such principles.

Now we move on to the books related to discovering hidden defects with hadeeth narrations, as this is a significant matter dealt with by the books of this science. Perhaps a hadeeth narration may have an excellent chain, clear in its soundness like the bright sun, but will nonetheless have a hidden defect. From the best of such books is *((Kitaab al-'Ilal)04-14)* by Ibn Abee Haatim which we have with us here. The book of hidden defect by *((ad-Darqutnee)04-36)* is considered the most comprehensive and excellent, but its printing has not been completed. The book *((al-'Ilal al-Kabeer)04-15)* by at-Tirmidhee has been organized and a commentary made of it. Also *((al-'Ilal as-Sagheer)04-16)* by at-Tirmidhee and which has an *((explanation of it)04-19)* by Haafidh Ibn Rajab which bears witness to his having traveled for knowledge. As for *((al-'Ilal)04-17)* by Imaam Ahmad it is restricted to hidden defects in biographies of narrators. As for *((al-'Ilal)04-18)* of 'Alee Ibn al-Madinee, there is only a small volume available from it. And from those books which are beneficial are *(('Awdhu' al-Bayaan)01-03)* which is a good book which can be benefited from as well as the book *((Jaame'a al-Usool)07-11)*. Likewise the book *((Sharh as-Sunnah)06-40)* by Baghawee is a good book which one can benefit from.

And also from the beneficial works in principles of jurisprudence are *(('Irshaad al-Fuhool)08-09)* and *((al-Mudhakirah)08-05)* by Sheikh ash-Shanqeetee. Sheikh al-Albaanee, may Allaah the Exalted preserve him said, "*The best of works in this subject is ((al-Ihkaam Fee Usool al-Ahkaam)08-02) by Ibn Hazm, may Allaah the Most High have mercy upon him.*" I am not calling you to become someone who adheres inflexibly to the Dhaaharee school, like Abu Muhammad Ibn Hazm was, but simply to benefit from his book, may Allaah reward him with good.

And from the valuable books is *((Tagleeq at-Ta'leeq FeeMaa Yata'leq Be al-Ahadeeth al-Mua'liqah Fee Saheeh al-Bukhaaree)02-33)* and *((ar-Risaalah)08-03)* by Imaam Shaafa'ee which is related to principles of jurisprudence, and *((al-Majmu'a)08-04)* by Imaam an-Nawawee, and *((al-Mughnee)07-07)* by Ibn Qudamah. Acquire these in order to benefit from them. But as for striving and struggling in some works over others, then this should be in the memorization of the Book of Allaah, and the memorization of the hadeeth of the Messenger of Allaah, may Allaah's praise and salutations be upon him and his household. But acquire these other books as references for yourself, so that if an issue is presented to you you can refer them.

There are hadeeth narrations which are well known and commonly said by the people. From them are narrations which are authentic at the highest level, from them are those which are authentic at an adequate intermediate level, from them are those which are weak, and from them are those which are fabricated or have no true basis to be considered hadeeth at all. Related to this are the following books: *((al-Maqaasid al-Hasnah Feemaa Ishtahar 'Alaa al-Alsanah)04-28)*, which is a valuable book. There is an author of a similar work, *((Kashf al-Kafaa' wa Mazeel al-Ilbaas 'Amaa 'Istahar 'Alaa Alsanah an-Nas)12-51)* who brings additional narrations and leaves some other mentioned narrations out. But *((al-Maqaasid al-Hasnah)04-28)* is better from the aspect that its author is an established scholar, whereas the author of *((Kashf al-Kafaa' wa Mazeel al-Ilbaa)12-51)* sometimes mentions a hadeeth narration which is completely false but doesn't mention anything further about this! An example of this is the false narration, [If difficult affairs come to you, then hold fast to the companions of the graves.] Similarly he mentions in his own introduction that it is possible for an individual to recognize the state of authenticity of a hadeeth- whether it is in fact authentic or whether it is weak- simply by mystical illumination or inspiration. Meaning that it will mystically become apparent to him that this narration is authentic, and this one is weak according to the scholars of hadeeth. That it will be revealed to him, just as Jibreel revealed revelation to the Prophet, may Allaah's praise and salutations be upon him and his household, and so that narration will be considered authentic or week! He also brings other corrupted beliefs in his introduction, corrupted beliefs that originate with the Sufees. There is also the book *((Asnaa al-Mutaalib fee Ahadeeth Mukhtalafahu al-Muraatib Min al-Ahaadeeth al-Mushtaharah)12-39)*.

We move on to the specific subject of books indicating fabricated hadeeth narrations, from among the most excellent of them is *((al-Maudhuaat)04-21)* by Ibn Jawzee, *((al-Abaateel)04-22)* by Jazqaanee, and *((al-Laa'lee al-Maudhuaat)04-20)* by Suyootee, which is a refutation of the assertions of the work *((al-Maudhuaat)04-21)* by Ibn Jawzee. Related to this last book is an examination of its own assertions entitled *((al-Fara'ed al-Majmu'ah)04-29)* by ash-Shawkaanee. However, this work almost does not clarify the conclusions of its investigations! How can this be? Consider an example: Imaam ash-Shawkaanee will mention the relevant hadeeth and then mention the stated position of Imaam as-Suyootee, but upon reading it an individual will not be able to determine whether ash-Shawkaanee agrees with as-Suyotee in his refutation of the claim of fabrication or agrees with the original assessment of Ibn Jawzee that the hadeeth is fabricated?!? However, Allaah allowed that an exemplary scholar, 'Abdur-Rahmaan al-Mu'alamee, may Allaah the Most High have mercy upon him, to comment and clarify the book by Imaam ash-Shawkaanee.

Also from the beneficial books is *((Dalaa'il an-Nabuwah)06-41)* by Imaam al-Bayhaqee, and *((Dalaa'il an-Nabuwah)06-42)* by Haafidh Abee Na'eem, may Allaah the Most High have mercy upon him. As for books related to the permissible abstinence from pursuing worldly goods, then from this works is *((Kitaab az-Zuhd)12-22)* by Imaam Ahmad, and *((az-Zuhd)12-23)* by Wakee'a *((az-Zuhd)12-24)* by Hinaad as-Saree *((Kitaab az-Zuhd)12-25)* by Ibn Mubaarak. And in the subject of Allaah's decree there is the beneficial book by Ibn Qayyim *((Shafa'a al-Aleel)06-28)*. As we have previously mentioned, you should be diligent in acquiring the books of Sheikh al-Islaam Ibn Taymeeyah and Haafidh Ibn Qayyim, within *((Majmu'a al-Fataawaa)07-19)* there is an entire volume related to this aspect of belief, meaning Allaah's decree. Now we proceed to the books which categorize the biographies of the different scholars, the works of tabaqat From them is *((at-Tabaqaat Ibn Sa'd)05-06)* as well as *((Tabaqaat al-Hufaadh)05-07)* by Haafidh as-Suyootee, there is also the book *((Tadhkirah al-Hufaadh)05-04)* by Haafidh adh-Dhahabee, from them is *((Tabaqaat ash-Shaafee'ah)05-08)* by as-Subkee and *((Tabaqaat al-Hanaabilah)05-09)* by Ibn Abee Ya'ala then *((Tabaqaat al-Hanaabilah)05-10)* by Ibn Rajab. There is also *((Minhaj al-Ahmad)05-16)* with biographies of those individuals upon the methodology of jurisprudence founded from the methodology of Imaam Ahmad. There is *((Tabaqaat al-Qura'a)05-11)* by Haafidh adh-Dhahabee, *((Tabaqaat an-Nahweeyeen)05-12)* *((Tabaqaat al-Mufassireen)05-13)* by Dawudee, and *((Tabaqaat al-Fuqahaa)05-14)*.

And from the generally important books is the book *((Shu'ab al-Emaan)02-10)* by Haafidh al-Bayhaqee, may Allaah, the Most High have mercy upon him, *((al-Umm)08-06)* by Shaafa'ee, *((Tabaqaat al-Khulafah)05-15)* by Ibn Khayyat, and the book *((al-Ba'ith wa an-Nashoor)05-22)*. Among the books of biography there is also the book *((al-Insaab)05-23)* by , and *((al-Kunyaa)05-24)* by Dawlaabee. Also from amongst the important books is *((Tufaat al-Ashraaf)04-30)* and *((al-Mu'ajam al-Mufahris)04-33)*.

As for those works which are books of heresy and misguidance, then those are the books of the Shee'ah, and the Ba'athees, and the books of Qadhafee, which may be found distributed at the book fair during some years. Unfortunately there is not the opportunity to enumerate them all and mention them completely. But also among the books of misguidance are those of the Sufis, and it is not proper that they be used and relied upon. The books of the Raafidhah, or the Shee'ah should also not be relied upon. Similarly those books which discuss general matters but which also excite and inflame people's nationalistic impulses and feelings should not be used or turned to. And the books written by those modern-day authors preceding upon new and recently devised ideas and concepts are not proper to be used or relied upon. Such as the book [[al-Aghaanee]] by Asfahaanee, which has been refuted by  the work *((Sayf al-Yamaanee Fee Nahr al-Asfahaanee)11-33)*. And that explanation of the Qur'aan [[Tafseer al-Manaar]] is considered from among the books of heresy and misguidance.

I mentioned some of these issues within the book *((Rudood Ahl-Ilm Alaa at-Taa'neen Fee Hadeeth as-Saher)11-25)* and have explained the great distance between the author of that explanation of the Qur'aan, Muhammad Rasheed Ridhaa, and the path of the first three generations, the Salaf. Additionally the books of Ibn 'Arabee such as [[al-Fusoos]], along with his explanations of the Qur'aan, are considered books of misguidance, as he is a deceiving Sufee who has committed a greater form of disbelief then the Christians and Jews. Therefore it is not proper that you use his books or the books of the later al-Ghazaalee, and I mean the present day Muhammad al-Ghazaalee, such as [[Dustoor al-Wahdah al-Thaqaafeeyah]], or such as the book [[Hummam ad-Da'eeyah]], and [[as-Sunnah an-Nabaweeyah Bayn Ahl al-Fiqh wa ahl-Hadeeth]]. Do not rely upon or use his books in any case.

And from the books of misguidance is the book [[Badaa'eea az-Zahoor]]; it is not a book to be used. Just as the book [[Tanbeeh al-Ghaafileen]] by Ibn Layth as-Samarkaandee also should not be. And the book [[Ayoon al-Mu'ajezaat]] by an evil wrongdoing Raafidhee, contains open and apparent disbelief in Islaam. The book [[al-Kaafee]] by Kulaynee is from this type of harmful book also, as well as the books [[as-Sunne al-Mutaalib fee Najaat Abee Taalib]], [[Saloonee Qabl In Tafqedoonee]], [[Matn al-Azhaar]], and [[Sharh alAzhaar]]. The book [[Tafseer az-Zamakhsharee]] is Mu'tazilee in nature and should not be used or relied upon. He is someone who is generally ignorant of the narrations of the Prophet. He authenticates those narrations which agree with his desires and he weakens those which do not conform to it.

And similarly the books of the people of biased partisanship; we have long been from those who warn against the books of such people. Hasan at-Turaabee is also someone who has produced books yet is an individual upon heresy and misguidance. Abu Rayyah, the author of [[Adhu'a Alaa as-Sunnah]]- and in reality this book is in fact "*darknesses upon the Sunnah*" not illuminations upon the Sunnah- is certainly astray and from the leading scholars of misguidance. The work [[Asha'aar al-Muqaaleh]] is not a book that should be relied upon; rather, within some of the poetry that he brings forth are statements of disbelief. Also from such books are the books related to sorcery such as [[Shams al-Ma'arif]] and the book [[ar-Rahmah]]. Therefore it is upon the student of knowledge to inquire and ask the people of knowledge which of the books he should purchase. From the harmful books are those of Ibn Alwaan, such as his book [[al-Mahjuraan]], as well as the publications by the author of [[Bayt al-Fiqh]], as he is a misguided false messiah from among the false messiahs. Certainly we've discussed some of his falsehood and nonsense within the work *((Irshaad Dhuwa al-Fatan Lil Iba'ad Ghulaat ar-Rawafidh min al-Yemen))11-17)*. Likewise the book [[Tabaqaat ash-Sha'raanee]] and [[al-Mizaan]] which he also wrote is from the books of misguidance and heresy.

Additionally those magazines which are published by the enemies of Islaam, or those works which are written by the people of biased partisanship- it is necessary that the student of knowledge distance himself from these books. The books of misguidance and harassment, as well as newspapers and magazines of a similar nature are not proper for the student of knowledge to busy himself with reading them. But as for the scholar who has the ability to refute their errors, then there is no harm in reading such works for the purpose of refuting them. And those books which advocate the celebration of the Prophet's a birthday in all the different forms and types- it is necessary to stay distant from them. Similarly the book [[Min al-Mahd Ilaa al-Lahd]] is from the books of heresy and misguidance. And from the books of disaster and calamity for the Muslims are those which are written by Yusuf Haashim ar-Raafa'ee which were printed by the people of Hudaydah, who consider themselves the 'Scholars of Yemen.' We say they are ignorant ones of Yemen, or the foolish ones of Yemen, we do not say or call them the scholars of Yemen. That statement is an insult and affront to all the people of Yemen, as thouigh they were upon such superstitious misguidance. Indeed the people of Yemen are free from any involvement in that misguidance which that book possesses. And it is necessary to bring forth a detailed explanation regarding such books; however the time does not permit that elaborate, detailed discussion

As for the books of Ibn Sinaa', then there is no harm in benefiting from those which are related to only medical science. But in relation to beliefs he is someone who denies the physical resurrection and so he is considered a heretical apostate. Indeed Sheikh al-Islaam Ibn Taymeeyah and Haafidh Ibn Qayyim stated that he was from among those who followed the worshipers of the ancient Egyptians. Additionally it should be said that the books of an-Nabahaanee are also from those books considered of misguidance and deviance from the religion. And now we will mention some of the beneficial books in the area of classical Islamic medical science, from among them is the book *((at-Tibb an-Nabawee)12-26)* by Haafidh Ibn Qayyim, which is a selection taken from his book *((Za'ad al-Ma'ad)09-05)*, as well as *((at-Tibb an-Nabawee)12-27)* by Haafidh adh-Dhahabee, and from them is *((at-Tibb an-Nabawee)12-28)* by as-Suyootee, as well as *((at-Tibb an-Nabawee)12-29)* by Abee Na'eem. There are also other general books of medical science from the Arabs which are proper to acquire and benefit from such as: *((al-Mu'atamid fee Tibb wa al-Hikmah)12-07)*. It contains some matters of misguidance as well as issues of deviation, but is suitable for the one who has the ability to distinguish between what is harmful and what is not. The work *((Mua'jiza'at as-Shifa'aa))12-19)* is also a good book.

And from the generally beneficial books is the book of our brother Muhammad Ibn 'Abdul-Wahaab al-'Abdalee al-Wasaabee *((al-Qawl al-Mufeed fee Adilat at-Tawheed))06-19)*... And from the beneficial books is the book *((Qaraa' Alasanah Fee Nafee at-Tataref wa al-Ghulu' wa aas-Shadhudh 'An Ahl Sunnah)11-19)* by our brother in Allaah's religion 'Abdul-'Azeez Ibn Yahya al-Bure'aa, may Allaah preserve him. And from the valuable books is the work *((al-'Itisaam)11-01)* by Shaatabee, and *((Bid'ah at-Ta'asub al-Madhhabee)11-15)* by our brother 'Eid Abbasee. And from the books which it is proper that you acquire is the book *((al-Ibtidaa' Fee Madhaar al-Ibtida'a')11-06)* And this is what Allaah has made easy for me to mention during this lecture and I was reminded of some of them by my brother in Allaah's religion, may Allaah reward him with good. And in closing, all praise is due Allaah, Lord of all the worlds.

*[FROM 'BRIDLING THE RESISTANT ONE': PAGE 492]*

# (33)

QUESTION REGARDING ACQUIRING THE
BOOKS WHICH ARE IMPORTANT FOR A
STUDENT OF KNOWLEDGE

nswer: Regarding the students of knowledge, than among their ranks there is the beginner who just has been mentioned by our noble brother, I ask Allaah, the Tremendous to grant him His blessings. And from among the students of knowledge there is also the one who has reached the level of researcher. As for the one who is a beginner, then we advise him to acquire the book *((Riyaadh as-Saaliheen)02-11)*, and to acquire *((Fath al-Majeed Sharh Kitaab at-Tawheed)06-12)* as well as *((al-'Ulu)06-45)* by Haafidh adh-Dhahabee, and its summarized version by Sheikh Muhammad Naassiruddeen al-Albaanee, as it is simpler to read, may Allaah reward him with good. As for the individual who is a beginner, I advise him to be diligent in striving to sit with the people of the Sunnah, as well as in asking them about the evidence of matters, asking them about anything that is not clear to him from the meanings of the Qur'aan, or which he does not understand from the hadeeth narrations of the Messenger of Allaah may the praise and salutations of Allaah be upon him, and that one mixes with the people who give importance to their religion. This will make him someone who is a student of knowledge and benefits from his efforts in a short amount of time; and that is something he would otherwise not know how to search for.

So attach yourself to your brothers from amongst the people of the Sunnah, either by means of the telephone, correspondence, or visiting your brothers. Because many of our brothers who fall short in traveling, they gather a number of questions and wait until one of their knowledgeable brothers comes to them. What is proper is that if an issue comes up they should travel in the path of Allaah for the sake of it. Then one is someone seeking knowledge even if it is for a single issue. This was the case of Jaabir Ibn 'Abdullah, who traveled to the land of Sham, north of Arabia, for the sake of a single issue, and for the sake of a single hadeeth narration. This hadeeth which he traveled for is well-known among our brothers who are students of knowledge. It is that of Riz Ibn Hubaish who asked Safwaan Ibn 'Asaal who said: "*There came this fountain of knowledge and asked him about a single issue!*" that being the matter of wiping over one's socks during purification. So what I intend by this is that if one travels for the sake of a single matter and that afterwards one achieves knowledge of that. After that, one would find another pleasure which also manifests itself within his mind as long as he is alive. But as for the likes of the books of those sects such as the Zaydeeyah, then I do not advise the beginner to get these and neither should the student of knowledge, whose time is limited and restricted.

Just take hold of the truths and do not worry yourself with those who oppose you. As for the one who wants to establish a library and wants to be able to research matters and write works, then it is still not for him to acquire such books, as he then takes them as a reference. However, the one who wishes to refute some of the innovations and contradictions to the truths which they contain within them should be the one to read them. A student of knowledge should give attention to that which will benefit him, as we have heard, such as the work *((Riyaadh as-Saaliheen)02-11)*, and *((Lu'lu wa al-Marjaan Fee Ma Itifaaq 'Aleihi ash-Shakhayn)02-16)*. Similarly, he should ask his brothers about beneficial books, just as it would be necessary for him to ask one who was an expert in a certain type of expensive merchandise if he wanted do purchase it from the market. The same is the case for books. One should ask the advice of the ones who have knowledge concerning them.

This is because in some books there are some matters which lie concealed like a poisonous scorpion, and that which is like a bloody death. So it is proper that one strives diligently to acquire those books which will benefit one and which will guide one upon the easiest way in the shortest amount of time. Do you not consider the one who reads and studies for twelve long years in the Haadee University? Their educational curriculum spans twelve years, yet even after that someone graduates and he himself admits that he is not able to stand in comparison to that student of knowledge who has studied the hadeeth sciences, because they simply repeat their various statements. They are not comparable to that student knowledge who studies in the Masjid al-Haram in Mecca. This is what day themselves say. But why? Because the one who studies by means of *"Allaah said,"* and *"The Messenger of Allaah said,"* may the praise and salutations of Allaah be upon him, gains significant benefits within a short time, in contradiction to the one who studies the various statements of men and studies the intricate issues upon which there are numerous disagreements, merely saying. [Muwedbillah says...] and [Abu Taalib says...], and [Abu al-Abbass says...] and [Yahya Ibn Hamzah says...] He has squandered his time, my brothers, especially if he was a beginner seeker of knowledge and especially if he was not someone with the ability to distinguish between the various evidences.

I will inform our brothers about myself, and I have told them of this on more than one occasion. In the beginning of my studies I would read from the book *((Rawdhat an-Naadher)08-08)*. I had resolved that I would not blame or take issue with any of those individuals mentioned in their differing. And I said, [Each of the people have some evidence, so why should you find fault with the people? Why should you do that when there are numerous statements?] I was someone who did not have the ability to distinguish between that which was evidence and that which was not considered evidence, or between that which was authentic evidence and that which was not authentic evidence. So I used to suppose that every statement I found had some evidence or, as is said amongst the people, that the [Differing among my

Ummah is a mercy.] Indeed Allaah is sufficient for us, and the sufficient Guardian! At that time I believed that every scholar who strove to independently derive a ruling was in some way correct, and that each of them had some support from the Messenger of Allaah! So therefore it is necessary, may Allaah bless you, to be diligent in taking from strong, valuable books. As for the researcher, it is not necessary that he acquire the work [[al-Bahr al-Zakhaar]] or other similar books. And we will stop here, May Allaah bless you all.

*[FROM 'ANSWERING THE QUESTIONER REGARDING THE MOST IMPORTANT ISSUES', PAGE 442]*

# (34)

QUESTION: WHAT BOOKS SHOULD A STUDENT OF KNOWLEDGE SHOULD BEGIN WITH, AND THEN WHICH SHOULD HE PROCEED ON TO?

nswer: As for the books that a beginning student of knowledge should start with- if he has the ability to read and write, he should read *((Fath al-Majeed Sharh Kitaab at-Tawheed)06-12)* as it is a tremendous book, as well as *((al-Aqeedatul-Wasateeyah)06-05)* of Sheikh al-Islaam Ibn Taymeeyah and *((al-Qawl al-Mufeed fee Adilat at-Tawheed))06-19)* of our brother Muhammad Ibn 'Abdul-Wahaab al-Wassabee. Likewise, he should read *((Bulugh al-Maraam)02-34)* and *((Riyaadh as-Saaliheen)02-11)* If he has read those books and wishes to proceed to other books, then if he has the ability he should begin memorizing the Qur'aan; this is better and preferable. Additionally, there is the issue of the Arabic language for our non-Arab brothers, which is essential. If a non-Arab is not strong in the Arabic language, then perhaps someone might go to him who has a pleasing form, outwardly reflecting Islaam, and explain the Qur'aan for him with other than its proper meaning and correct explanation. This is known to be what happened with the misguided sect known as the Mu'tazilah.

*[FROM 'EXCELLENT RESPONSES TO QUESTIONS FROM THOSE PRESENT AND THOSE ABSENT': PAGE 156]*

# (35)

QUESTION: IN THE NAME OF ALLAAH, THE MOST GRACIOUS, THE MOST MERCIFUL. I HAVE COME HERE ONLY FOR A SHORT TRIP AND A SHORT TIME  I AM NOT ABLE TO REMAIN HERE AND ACQUIRE KNOWLEDGE FROM THE HAND OUR ESTEEMED SHEIKH AND FROM THE HANDS OF THOSE OTHERS WHO TEACH HERE. FOR THAT REASON I ASK OUR SHEIKH WITH WHAT HE ADVISES ME IN REGARD TO BOOKS TO READ AND STUDY, AND ESPECIALLY IN THE SCIENCE OF HADEETH?

nswer: That which I recommend or advise the brother with is that if he reaches the point where he has a good understanding through reading, he should read works such as *((Saheeh al-Bukhaaree)02-01)*, *((Saheeh Muslim)02-02)*, and *((Tafseer Ibn Katheer)01-01)*. If his level of understanding is below this, than I advise him to frequently read from *((Riyaadh as-Saaliheen)02-11)* and *((Lu'Lu' wa al-Marjaan Feemaa 'Itifaaq 'Aleihi as-Sheikhaan)02-16)*, as well as *((Fath al-Majeed Sharh Kitaab at-Tawheed)06-12)*. In the subject of fiqh, to read from the book *((Bulugh al-Maraam)02-34)* of Haafidh Ibn Hajr. Knowledge is that which calls one and invites one further. When one reads from *((Bulugh al-Maraam)02-34)* it will indicate to him other reference works which he then refers to. Likewise, when you read from the work *((Lu'Lu' wa al-Marjaan Feemaa 'Itifaaq 'Aleihi as-Sheikhaan)02-16)*, at times they will indicate other reference works in some of its narrations mentioned without the full chain. I also advise the brothers to invite and facilitate attendance of a knowledgeable brother from among our brothers here who were students, so that perhaps they will instruct them in the religion, purely seeking Allaah's face and His reward for one, two, or three months. This time is like a school established by the favor of Allaah, in which his study for the sake of Allaah, and for the purpose that he might read from some works related to the Arabic language such as *((Tuhfat as-Sunneyah)10-07)* until his tongue becomes trained and he gains understanding of the meanings of words. Simply reading from books is not the same as taking knowledge from a scholar, even though those books which we of mentioned will benefit by the permission of Allaah, the Most High.

Before this there is the matter of memorizing what is easy for you from the Qur'aan, as the Qur'aan is considered to be that which heals and rectifies the illnesses and diseases of our hearts and our bodies. *Verily, this Qur'aan guides to that which is most just and right*-(Surah al-Isra':9)   The Companions of the Messenger of Allaah, may Allaah be pleased with them all, would learn the Qur'aan when they embraced Islaam. Some of them said, "*We use to learn emaan before the Qur'aan, and we would not proceed until we had fully learned ten verses...*" or a statement which carries this meaning. So one should first be fully engaged with the study of the Qur'aan and thereafter with the study of these other books. Whenever different life matters occur, then it is possible for one to refer them back to the relevant books. For instance, the issue of divorce. Regarding this you would refer to *((Nayl al-Awtaar)03-08)* and *((Subl as-Salaam)03-06)* by Sana'anee. It strengthens and fortifies an individual when he searches for the guidance regarding a matter himself. Then he is confident and has assured himself that the ruling is not simply the statement of so-and-so, or the opinion of so-and-so. However, if you have searched and found the true ruling of a matter, then know that the Messenger of Allaah, may Allaah's praise and salutations be upon him, said, as was mentioned in the narration of Ibn 'Abbaas, *{Being informed of something is not like observing it oneself.}* [1]  And as a poet once said:

> *Oh Ibn al-Karaam, will you not draw close to observe, as reflecting upon,*
>
>> *that which has occurred in  front of your own eyes is not like hearing about it.*

The one who is able to go to the land of the two holy sanctuaries of Mecca and Medinahh, or to this place, in order to sit with the scholars of the people of the Sunnah, then indeed I advise them with such sittings with the people of the Sunnah. Sitting with the people of innovation in the religion does not result in or lead to anything other than misguidance. Similarly, sitting with the people of bias and <u>partisanship to</u> different groups and movements amongst

[1]

the Muslims also does not result in or lead to anything other than misguidance. Indeed, sitting with these people of bias and partisanship causes destruction to knowledge, as perhaps an person was someone who had memorized the Qur'aan, but when he entered into this way of partisanship, he became forgetful of that which he had memorized, and his understanding and thinking became corrupted, when previously it was straight and steadfast. And we end with the praise of Allaah, Lord of all the Worlds.

*[FROM 'A DEFENDING MISSION FROM AUDIO LECTURES UPON THE PEOPLE OF IGNORANCE & SOPHISTRY': VOL. 1, PAGE 118]*

# (36)

QUESTION: WHAT ARE THE MOST AUTHENTIC BOOKS THROUGH WHICH WE KNOW FROM THE TRANSMITTED ACCOUNTS FROM THE LIVES OF THE SUCCESSORS OF THE COMPANIONS?

nswer: Reading books in this subject requires that an individual have understanding of the sciences related to recognizing the reliability of individual who transmit reports and accounts. As these books mention hadeeth narrations and different stories with their original chains of narrations, such that it is them required that you read biographies in *((al-Hilyah)05-03)*, and *((Tareekh ad-Dimashq)09-10)*, and *((Taarikh Baghdaad)09-03)*, and within *((Kaamel)05-25)* of Ibn 'Adee, and *((adh-Dhua'faa')05-26)* of 'Uqaylee. So there is not present any such book that we can simply say:

[This is the most authentic book in this subject, and everything within it is authentic.] As you might find that there is a story that circulated, spread, and become widely known among the people, and the Khateebs all move their heads when mentioning it, yet it is not authentically verified as coming from that Sucessor to the Companions. I advice my brother who wishes to gain awareness of the life stories of the Successors of the Companions to read within books such as: *((Seyaar)05-17)* by Haafidh adh-Dhahabee and I refer to *((Seyaar 'Alaam an-Nubala')05-17)*. And read within the works such as *((Tadhkirat al-Hufaadh)05-04)*, and such as *((Taarikh al-Kabeer)05-27)* by adh-Dhahabee. As it was his practice, may Allaah have mercy upon him, to criticize the veracity of some narrated stories and accounts because of them not being affirmed and authentic, as such his books are considered from the best and most authentic of such works.

*[FROM 'A DEFENDING MISSION FROM AUDIO LECTURES UPON THE PEOPLE OF IGNORANCE & SOPHISTRY': VOL. 1 PAGE 387]*

# (37)

QUESTION:  WHAT IS YOUR VIEW OF
THE BOOK 'FIQH AS-SUNNAH' BY
SAYYED SAABIQ?

nswer: It is generally acceptable, however it often relies upon weak hadeeth. Additionally its discussion of the issue of shaving the beard shouldn't be given any consideration, nor the issue discussing the person whose work is strenuous- as he incorrectly allows him to eat and not fast and then perform an expiation for this. This is not correct. For in the time of the Prophet, may Allaah's praise and salutations be upon him, there were those who whose work was strenuous and it was possible for someone to work while fasting. We used to work strenuously in Ramadhaan while we were in Saudi Arabia.

They say that he is one those scholars of Egypt who many of the people follow and adhere to. However as for the book, it contains those shortcoming that are know to be within it. Also I have seen within it very good statements in regarding the matter of insurance, and he is to be thanked for this. As I have benefited from that discussion, may Allaah reward him with good. However in general it is not to be relied upon as a work. Superior in value to it is the book *((Nayl al-Awtaar)03-08)* or the work *((Subl as-Salaam)03-06)* of Imaam Sanaanee, or the book *((ar-Rabaa'ee)07-12)*. He is one of the scholars from the scholars of Yemen. Also a more excellent work is *((al-Muntaqaa)12-21)* by the grandfather of Sheikh al-Islaam Ibn Taymeeyah, who is named either 'Abdul-Haleem or 'Abdul-Salam.

Accordingly, anyone less than a student of knowledge must refer back to a scholar in his country from what he sees of that which is contrary to what is known to be true from that which is in the book, and to not rely on it alone.

*[FROM 'THE FINAL TRAVELS OF THE IMAAM OF THE ARAB PENINSULA' BY UMM SALAMAH AS-SALAFEEYAH: PAGE 233]*

# (38)

QUESTION: WHAT DO YOU SAY ABOUT A STUDENT OF KNOWLEDGE WHO ENCOURAGES BEGINNING STUDENTS OF KNOWLEDGE TO READ THE BOOK [[FEE DHILAAL AL-QUR'AAN]] AND TO PLACE IT WITHIN THEIR HOMES? I EXPLAINED TO THIS STUDENT THAT THESE STUDENTS ARE ONLY BEGINNING STUDENTS OF KNOWLEDGE AND THEY DO NOT HAVE THE ABILITY TO DISTINGUISH BETWEEN THE BENEFICIAL AND HARMFUL STATEMENTS IN THIS BOOK, OR DISCERN WHAT THE AUTHOR STATED REFLECTING THE CONCEPT OF UNITY OF THE CREATOR AND THE CREATION! I PUT FORTH THAT THEY SHOULD READ BOOKS SUCH AS 'FATH AL-BAAREE', 'SHARH AL-MUSLIM' AND 'RIYAADH AS-SAALIHEEN', BUT HE CHALLENGED THIS SAYING, "THESE BOOKS ALSO HAVE MISTAKES AND ERRORS. SO WHY CAN THEY READ THOSE BOOKS AND NOT READ THIS BOOK?" I RESPONDED BY SAYING: "BUT HE HAS STATEMENTS ADVANCING THE CONCEPT OF THE UNITY OF THE CREATOR WITH THE CREATION!" HOWEVER, HE REPLIED: "WHAT ELSE IS THERE OTHER THAN THIS ONE THING?" AS HE DOES NOT SEE THIS ISSUE AS SIGNIFICANT ENOUGH. SO ARE THE FOLLOWING ACTIONS HE IS DOING CORRECT?

FIRSTLY, ADVISING THE STUDENTS TO READ THAT BOOK, MEANING [[FEE DHALEEL AL-QUR'AAN]]. SECONDLY, MAKING EQUAL THE AUTHOR OF THAT BOOK TO THE TWO IMAAMS, IMAAM AN-NAWAWEE, AND IMAAM IBN HAJR IN REGARD TO: A) MISTAKES IN THE ISSUES OF BELIEF, AS WELL AS B) THEIR POSITION AMONG THE PEOPLE OF KNOWLEDGE.

nswer: As for the book [[Fee Dhaleel al-Qur'aan]], and the other books of Sayyed Qutb, may Allaah have mercy upon him, then I advise that they should not be read. As some of the Muslim groups who have fallen into the innovation of declaring other Muslims as disbelievers developed, and some of the young Muslim men have become individuals with the same corrupt beliefs as those misguided groups, due to some of the incorrect expressions and statements of Sayyed Qutb, may Allaah have mercy upon him. Yet Sayyed Qutb should only be considered a writer, but not a scholar capable of explaining the Qur'aan. As his explanation of the Qur'aan is a personal explanation coming from someone who for 11 years, lived in the state of disbelieving denial of Allaah! How could such a person be considered suitable to write an explanation of the Qur'aan?! However it is those callers from the organization of the "Muslim Brotherhood" whose practice it is to identify individuals as having an elevated status even if they do not in fact qualify for that status. For example: They say, [The professor said], and [The professor such and such...] Yet in reality he is only someone who falsely inflames and agitates the people's sentiments, and not in fact a professor.

When we attended the Islamic University in Medinah, even if you or someone who was highly distinguished in knowledge and understanding, they would say to you: "Have you read the book, [[Allaah]], [[ar-Rasool]], [[al-Islaam]] by Sa'eed Hawaa?" And if you had said that you had not read these books, then they would say to you: [You do not possess anything of knowledge.].

Yet we, all praise is due to Allaah, indeed embraced seeking knowledge from that knowledge which was truly beneficial. And I ask Allaah. the Tremendous to preserve our brother Rabee'a Ibn Haadee as he clarified and exposed the incorrect beliefs held by Sayyed Qutb, and those matters which he was upon a deviation from the truth. And similar to this was the clarifying effort of our brother, may Allaah have mercy upon him, 'Abdullah Ibn Muhammad ad-Duwaysh who was a strong memorizer in the sciences of hadeeth, the like of which I have not seen someone similar to him. As within his book *((al-Mawrood al-'Adhab az-Zalaal Fee Bayaan Akhtaa' adh-Dhalaal)11-26)* he is indicated many issues which were mistakes by Sayyed Qutb.

So Sayyed Qutb should not be considered from those who could properly explain the meaning of Qur'aan, nor amongst those who have distinguished themselves in the level of knowledge they acquired. Rather he was an individual who had tremendous enthusiasm for Islaam, but without sound understanding. I advise the brothers to return to utilizing *((Tafseer Ibn Katheer)01-01)* regarding which Imaam ash-Shawkaanee may Allaah have mercy on him, stated: *"He is explanation of the Qur'aan is from among the best of explanations, if not the best of them."* And Suyootee, stated in his work *((Tabaqaat al-Huffadh)05-04)* *"Certainly Tafseer Ibn Katheer is from among the best of explanations of the Qur'aan."* As *((Tafseer Ibn Katheer)01-01)* is an explanation of the Qur'aan through the Qur'aan itself, as well as the authentic prophetic narrations. It clarifies that which is authentic from the Sunnah from that which is not authentic, and that which has a hidden weakness from that which has been transmitted soundly without defect or having been altered by unsupported stories originating from the reports coming from previous nations of the Christians and Jews. And similarly I advise you to read those explanations which come from our first generations such as *((Tafseer Ibn Jareer)01-04)* *((Tafseer al-Baghawee)01-07)* and what is available from *((Tafseer Ibn Abee Haatim)01-08)* and *((Tafseer Ibn Mardaweeh)01-09).* As they contain tremendous benefit and good. But do not rely upon [[Fee Dhaleel]] as I fear that it will lead you into misguidance. And it it is somehow necessary that you read it then, I advise that you read it along with the books of clarification by the brother 'Abdullah Ibn Muhammad ad-Duwaysh and with the books written by Sheikh Rabee'a Ibn Haadee, may Allaah preserve him.

*[FROM 'ADVICES & CLARIFICATIONS': PAGES 63-66]*

# (39)

QUESTION: WHAT KNOWLEDGE RELATED BENEFITS CONNECTED TO UNDERSTANDING THE RELIGION PROPERLY CAN BE FOUND IN THE BOOK 'IRWAA AL-GHALEEL'?

nswer: The work *((Irwaa al-Ghaleel)04-32)* is a book containing rulings and explanations of how to implement the religion, and it contains criticism and praise of hadeeth narrators, as well as clarifying authentic narrations from weak ones. It is considered from the most valuable books of Sheikh al-Albaanee, may Allaah, the Most High preserve him. Additionally, it collects the various paths of narrations which the Sheikh found at that time, which is perhaps something which was not easy for someone in our age. Therefore it is from the most prized works. I do not say the most prized from the works of the Sheikh, rather from the most prized or valuable of all the books available. And how many different authors there are in this age who have benefited from the books of the Sheikh, may Allaah preserve him!

*[FROM 'A DEFENDING MISSION FROM AUDIO LECTURES UPON THE PEOPLE OF IGNORANCE & SOPHISTRY': VOL. 2, PAGE 69]*

# (40)

**N**OTES REGARDING THE BEST BOOKS TAKEN FROM THE STATEMENTS OF SHEIKH MUQBIL, MAY ALLAAH HAVE MERCY UPON HIM

(POINTS 70-90 ONLY)

**H**e used to say:

70- The best book after the book of Allaah, the Most High and the Most Exalted, explaining the matter of worshipping Allaah alone is the book *((Fath al-Majeed)06-12)*.

71- The best book in the area of various rulings derived from the source texts is *((Nayl al-Awtaar)03-08)*.

72- The best book which gathered rulings in the religion is *((Majmua' al-Fatawaa)07-19)* of Sheikh al-Islaam Ibn Taymeeyah.

73- The best book in refutation of the matter of magic and witchcraft is *(Miftah Dar as-Saadah)11-27)* by Ibn Qayyim.

74- The best book related to the medicine of the Prophet is *((Tibb an-Nabawee)12-26)* taken from the writings of Ibn Qayyim found within *((Zaad al-Ma'ad Fee Haadee Khair al-Ebaad)09-05)* which can be purchased as an individual volume.

75- The best book dealing with and explaining the harms resulting from sins is the book *((al-Jawaab al-Kaafee Liman Sa'ill An Ad-Duwaa' Ash-Shaa'fee)12-30)* by Ibn Qayyim.

76- From among the best books which deal with the merits of the Companions are *((al-Ahaad wa al-Muthanee)09-08)* by Ibn Abee 'Assim, the book *(al-'Isaabah)05-02)*, and the book *((Fadhaa'il as-Sahabah)05-30)* by Mustapha al-Adawee.

77- The book *((al-Maqasid al-Husna')03-28)* is better than the book *((Kashf al-Khafaa')12-09)*, as the writer of 'Kashf al-Khafaa' gathers narrations from different places of varying value, as well as even taking some from the work *((al-Maqasid al-Husna')03-28)* itself.

78- The best book is the branch of knowledge in the Arabic language known as 'eloquence' is *(('Aqood al-Jamaan)12-10)*.

79- The *((book of Ibn Azuuz)07-09)* refuting of the some of the adherents to the Maalakee school of jurisprudence in the issue of raising one's hands in ritual prayer is from the best of books in its subject.

80- *((The best book)12-11)* authored on the subject of major sins is by a modern day author whose name is Abu al-Bara' (Ghassan al-Philistinee), and after it the classical book *((al-Zuwaajir An Iqtiraaf al-Kabaa'ir)12-12)* by al-Haithamee.

81- The best book authored in the matter of belief regarding our seeing Allaah on the Day of Resurrection is the *((book of Darqutnee)06-50)*, and after it take from what has been summarized of this from Ibn Qayyim, may Allaah have mercy upon him, in his book *((Haadee al-Arwaah' ila Balad al-Afraah)06-51)*.

82- The best book written in the subject of sending prayers when hearing the name of the Prophet Muhammad, may Allaahs' praise and salutation be upon him and his family, is the book *((Jalaa' al-Afhaam)12-15)* by Ibn Qayyim, despite the fact that it does contains some weak hadeeth. Similarly, the *((book of as-Sakhawee)12-16)*. Yet it is to be considered as second in value to the book of Ibn Qayyim. It also contains weak hadeeth, yet contains good knowledge-related benefits.

83- The best book written regarding the subject of travelling specifically to the grave of the Messenger, may Allaah's praise and salutation be upon him and his family, is the book *((as-Saaram al-Mankee fee Rad alaa as-Subkee)06-52)*.

84- The best book authored regarding the detailed characteristics of the Hajj of the Prophet, may Allaah's praise and salutation be upon him and his family, is *((Hajj al-Wadaa'a)07-10)* by Ibn Hazm, and likewise what is found in *((Zaa'd al-Ma'd)09-05)* by Ibn Qayyim, as well as what Ibn Hazm related on the subject in his work *((al-*

*Muhalaa)08-07).*

85- The best book written in refutation of the sect of the Raafidhah is *((Minhaj as-Sunnah)11-09)* of Sheikh al-Islaam Ibn Taymeeyah.

86- The Sheikh, may Allaah have mercy upon him, said, *"The book of Sheikh al-Islaam Ibn Taymeeyah, may Allaah have mercy upon him, ((Iqtida' as-Siraat al-Mustaqeem)11-02) is a truly tremendous book."*

87- The best reference source for the narrations from the first generations is *((Mussanaf Abee Bakr Ibn Abee Shaibah)02-14)*, then the *((Mussanaf of Abdal-Razzaq as-Sannanee)02-15)*, and then *((Tafseer at-Tabaree)01-04)*.

88- The best book dealing with the correct understanding of Allaah's name an-Nuzul, is the book of Sheikh al-Islaam Ibn Taymeeyah: *((Ismuhu An-Nuzul)06-53)*.

89- The book *((ad-Dur al-Manthur)01-06)* by as-Suyutee is the best book in relation to what it gathers together of narrations explaining the Qur'aan. However, in regard to the overall level of authenticity of the narrations it contains, it includes accepted narrations, the highest grade of accepted narrations, weak narrations, and narrations that are actually fabricated.

90- The book *((Makhraj Min al-Fitnah)11-12)* and the book *((Sayyuf al-Baaterah)11-20)* contains that which I recommend to the students of knowledge.

*[FROM THE EXPEDITIONS OF SHEIKH MUQBIL IBN HAADEE AL-WAADI'EE WHEN CALLING TO ALLAAH, PAGES 121-123]*

# (41)

SOME BENEFICIAL NOTES REGARDING BOOKS

he author Abu Hamaam said: Certainly Abu 'Abdur-Rahman, may Allaah have mercy upon him, was one who read extensively and he possessed subtle expertise in relation to books, their benefits, and their authors, and similarly the same insight regarding the books of the people of innovation in the religion. Certainly the student of knowledge loves to know those books which the scholars have warned us about, as well as those that they have advised us towards and recommended. So the following are the books that our sheikh warned from, or praised and recommended, or explained a matter regarding their authors or pointed out some of their benefits. So I say and the success is from Allaah. Abu 'Abdur-Rahman, may Allaah have mercy upon him said:

*Benefit:* The book of [[al-Munfalutee]] is not to be relied upon.

*Benefit:* The book which is an explanation *((Riyaadh as-Saaliheen)02-11)* which is titled [[Daleel al-Faalheen]] is an explanation based upon the beliefs of the innovated Asha'ree sect, so you should be warned from it.

*Benefit:* Imaam Nawawee included weak hadeeth narrations in his book *((Riyaadh as-Saaliheen)02-11)* incorrectly relying upon the lack of comment of Imaam Abu Dawud or that of Imaam at-Tirmidhee as an affirmation of their authenticity, from that included in their own hadeeth compilations.

*Benefit:* The book [[Ilm as-Shaamekh]] which was written by al-Muqbilee supports and advocates the innovated views of the Asha'ree sect against the way of Ahlus-Sunnah, he has enmity towards those who raise up the way of Ahlus-Sunnah in opposition to the Shee'ah, and he does not restrict himself to the methodology of the people of the Sunnah. He falsely states: [Dhahabee had hatred towards members of the Prophet's household] and he says [And those people of hatred for the family of the Prophet from the region of Shaam-north of the Arabian peninsula- such as ad-Dhaabhee...] And attacks Imaam Bukharee severely, simply because he authored the book *((Khalq Afa'al al-Ibaad)06-33)*.

*Benefit:* The best printed edition of *((Tareekh al-Kabeer)05-21)* by Imaam al-Bukhaaree is the one with the verification by Imaam al-Mu'alamee.

*Benefit:* The majority of *((explanation the Qur'aan)01-08)* from Ibn Abee Hatim has been lost to us, having not reached our time. However I viewed a surviving volume of it in the library in the Sanctuary in Mecca.

*Benefit:* If Ibn Adee mentions in his book *((al-Kamal)05-25)* hadeeth narrations from an individual narrator indicating his different narrations, and defends him as a narrator, then he considers him a reliable narrator. But if he mentions an individual and simply mentions that he is the only one who related this specific narration, then this is not considered an affirmation of reliability from him. As indeed Suyutee stated that "*The mentioning of a hadeeth of Ibn 'Adee in his work ((al-Kamal)05-25) is enough for it to be considered weak.*"

*Benefit:* The books of Sheebat al-Hamd are not to be relied upon.

*Benefit:* The books of Saaboonee, all of them, are not to be relied upon, as he is a sufi and a bigoted biased follower of the Hanafee school of jurisprudence. The people of knowledge have made clear his misguidance and deviation.

*Benefit:* As for the author of *((Tafseer Jalalayn)01-10)*, he is someone who lacks clarity of understanding. In once place he will explain 'Allaah's rising above his throne' with the false metaphorical meaning of "having conquered," and in another place he brings the correct understanding which has been transmitted from the first generations of Muslims in affirmation of its reality. He also has some aspects of the beliefs of the sect of the Mu'tazilah.

*Benefit:* book The book [[al-'Aql]] by Dawud al-Muhbar is one which has been criticized by the scholars.

*Benefit:* The book *((Aqeedatul as-Salaf)06-54)* by Abee 'Uthmaan as-Saboonee is one I advise reading.

*Benefit:* The book *((al-Qadr)06-55):* the people of knowledge differ as to whether its authorship is correctly attributed to Imaam Maalik or to the scholar Ibn Wahb.

*Benefit:* There is an *((excellent treatise)12-14)* by Sheikh Muhammad as-Sabeel discussing the prohibition of obtaining American citizenship for those who are not originally American.

*Benefit:* The book [[al-Mubaas fee Tafseer Ibn Abbaas]] cannot be affirmed to Ibn Abbaas, as within its chain of transmission there are several defects. There is a narrator, Muhammad Ibn Marwaan as-Sadee, who is accused of fabrications narrations, and he narrates on Muhammad Ibn as-Saa'ib al-Kalbee who was one who fabricated narrations, who lastly transmitted this work from Abee Saalah Baatham and he is a weak narrator.

*Benefit:* The first book to discuss the heretical sects who left Islaam by their deviation and expose them was the *((book)11-29)* by Abu Muhammad al-Yemenee, and it is its author's best work.

*Benefit:* As for the book [[Tooq al-Hamaamalı]] attributed to Abu Muhammad Ibn Hazm, then we neither deny nor affirm this attribution. All we say is that the scholars mentioned n the book are in fact known to be the scholars of Abu Muhammad Ibn Hazm.

*Benefit:* The book [[Kashf]] by Zamakhsharee, ends the discussion of every surah of the Qur'aan with a weak, unauthentic hadeeth.

*Benefit:* The book *((Fadha'il al-Qur'aan)12-56)* mentions for every surah those hadeeth which discuss its specific merits. It has two chains of transmission. The first is through Maseerah Ibn 'Abd Rabuhu, and the second through

Nuh Ibn Abee Marayam.

*Benefit:* As for the book [[Fee Dhaleeel al-Qur'aan]] then Muhammad 'Ameen al-Misree has informed me that certainly those groups who indiscriminately declare the Muslims to be disbelievers discuss and debate with it, and that they derive rulings and understanding from it and from the other books of Sayyed Qutb, may Allaah have mercy upon him.

*Benefit:* The book of commentary of the Qur'aan *((Fath al-Qadeer)01-05)* has the best discussion of the separated Arabic letters found within the Qur'aan, to the best of my knowledge. And it is a remarkable explanation in that it challenges blind following, as its compiler states his evidenced position even when that clearly differs from what most of the people state.

*Benefit:* The book [[Tanaasiq Bayn al-Ayaat]] discusses the harmony of different verses of the Qur'aan. The first one to write a work in this subject was al-Bagaa'ee. Ash-Shawkaanee stated, "*This knowledge is not from the Sharee'ah of Islaam, and its discussion should not be entered into.*" And I say yes, his assessment of it is correct.

*Benefit:* The books of Sheikh Ihsaan Elaayhee Dhaheer exposed the truth of the sect of the Rafidhaah. It was asked of him that he should not publish his books. He said, "*I agree, upon the condition that you burn and destroy all those books (of misguidance) which I quoted from in my books.*" They said to him, "*That is not possible!*"

*Benefit:* The book [[Islaam and Christianity]] by 'Abdullah al-Qaseemee, contains a refutation of some of the claims of the Raafidhah. Its author had once been upon Islaam, and then he deviated, falling into apostasy.

*Benefit:* As for the book *((Kitaab at-Tawheed)06-36)* by Ibn Khuzaymah- he made it a condition of the work that he would only include authentic narrations, but it contains some weak narrations, as he is a scholar of hadeeth who was somewhat lax in his grading of hadeeth, both him and his well-known student Ibn Hibaan.

*Benefit:* The book [[Haqaa'iq al-Tafseer]] by Muhammad Ibn al-Hasan Abu 'Abdur-Rahman as-Salamee who was from the scholars of Imaam al-Bayhaqee. But the people of knowledge have stated, "*If he believed that which he stated in his explanation of the Qur'aan, then he has disbelieved, and what he has written is from misguidance.*"

*Benefit:* The book *((al-'Ilaal al-Kabeer)04-15)* by at-Tirmidhee, which is organized as part of his *((Jaamae')02-06)* collection. Whereas the separate work *(al-'Ilaal as-Sagheer)04-16)* is that which Ibn Rajab has written a *((commentary)04-19)* and explanation of.

*Benefit:* The book *((Hajjatul Wadaa')07-10)* by Ibn Hazm has been verified by 'Abdul-Majeed ash-Shamree with a good verification. Someone else verified this book before he did, but his verification is better that the first one.

*Benefit:* the book *((Shafaa' al-Ileel)09-01)* by Qadhee Ayaadh is a valuable book, even if he derives some matters from weak narrations, or fabricated narrations. Still, the book in its entirety is not weak or fabricated, because he was a scholar of the hadeeth sciences.

*Benefit:* I advise reading the Book *((at-Tawheed)06-56)* by Ibn Munduh.

*Benefit:* The book *((al-'Irhaab)11-30)* is a good book, and we were astonished at these books of refutation of the people of innovation in Islaam. As for the book *((al-Qutubiyyah)11-17)* then I say about it what I said about the first book. And we of heard good about the author of the first book, Zayd al-Madhkhalee, but as for the author of the second book- then I do not know him.

*Benefit:* Regarding the scholastic discussion surrounding the issue of reciting the "basmallah" aloud, then treatises have been written regarding it by al-Darqutnee, who adhered to the Shaafa'ee school of jurisprudence, and Khateeb al-Baghdadee, who did also. Likewise Ibn 'Abdul-Barr wrote regarding this issue, as did Ibn Jawzee.

*Benefit:* As for those mentioned books by Hasan al-Banna, as-Saba'ee, and Muhammad al-Ghazaalee, then we do not have time to read them even if they are said to be refutations against those who have innovated in the religion. Marwaan said, *"Do not place one's confidence in three: the innovator who refutes another innovator, the one whose focus is narrating stories, and the one who has adopted the innovated path of Sufism."*, as today they will criticize him, yet tomorrow they might praise him.

*Benefit:* If you read from all of the ignorant books of the twentieth century, you will not gain anything of significance. Rather, I advise you to take the book *((at-Tawasul wa al-Waseelah)06-49)* of Ibn Taymeeyah and its like.

*Benefit:* The book *((al-Qaa'edah Jaleelah fe at-Tawasul wa al-Waseelah)06-49)* contains some expressions and statements that require further clarification, but is considered one of the reference works in this subject of intercession between the creation and Allaah. The similar *((book by Sheikh al-Albaanee )06-57)* is easier to comprehend, while the work of Ibn Taymeeyah is more extensive and thorough in its knowledge-based discussion.

*Benefit:* The hadeeth narrations which come from the sect of the Zaydeeyah are not accepted, nor those of the sect of the Karamateh. And from their well-known works are [[al-Amaalee]] and [[Shams al-Akhbaar]], both of which originate with Yahyaa Ibn al-Hasan.

*Benefit:* I do not advise you to read the books of Sayyed Qutb, the books of Muhammad al-Ghazaalee, the books of Muhammad Qutb, or the books of Zaynab al-Ghazaalee. May Allaah reward our brother Rabee'a with good, as certainly he has advised and clarified that which is deviation from the truth and misguidance found in the books of Sayyad Qutb.

*Benefit:* The book *((ar-Ru'yaah)06-50)* by ad-Darqutnee: I do not know of a work comparable to it in this subject, because in it he proceeds upon the methodology of the scholars of hadeeth. Also his book *((Haadee al-Arwaah)06-51),* even though it is not specific to the subject of affirming that the believers will see Allaah. Its attribution to him is correct, because the scholars within the chains mentioned for it are the scholars of Imaam ad-Darqutnee.

*Benefit:* The work *((Meezaan al-'Itidaal)05-19)* by Dhahabee is one in which he compiles the biographies according to the standards of what was the truth and what was false; whatever was the truth regarding a narrator he accept and whatever was false regarding a narrator, he rejected.

*Benefit:* al-Haakim compiled his work *((Mustradrak)02-25)* at the very end of his life.

*Benefit:* As for the book [[al-'Elaan]] by Zarkulee, then its author has an inclination towards the organization the Muslim Brotherhood, and so he should not be relied upon. He praises them, and from what is apparent is from their ranks.

*Benefit:* The book of Sh. at-Tuwayjeree *((Fee Rad 'Alaa man Yaqool: In al-'Ardh Tadur)11-31)* is one which must be in the hands of the student of knowledge. It is a refutation against Mahmood as-Sawaaf.

*Benefit:* The work *((Fatawaa Umar Ibn- 'Abdul-'Azeez)07-08)* is from the best collections of the statements of the generation which came after the Companions of the Prophet, except in the matter of failing to distinguish what is authentically narrated from what is weak in narration.

*Benefit:* The book *((Jalaa' al-Afhaam)12-15)* by Ibn Qayyim is the best book written about the subject of the excellence of sending prayers upon him when hearing the name of the Prophet Muhammad, may Allaah's praise and salutation be upon him and his family.

*Benefit:* the Book [[ar-Rawdh al-Basaam Fee adh-Dhab 'An Sunnah Abee Qaasim]] by Ibn Wazeer is an abridged version of al-'Awaasem wa al-Qawaasim. In it he explicitly states his beliefs as a Muslim and indicates that he was afflicted by having been affected by having a brother from the sect of the Shee'ah.

*Benefit:* As for the book *((al-'Asmaa' wa al-Sifaat)06-35)* by al-Bayahaqee, then he was in some degree influenced by the incorrect beliefs of his sheikh, Ibn Farook, in what he wrote. But as for his book *((al-'Itiqaad)06-59)* then in this work he fully proceeded upon and explained the methodology of the first generations in essential beliefs.

*Benefit:* The work *((Ta'weel Mukhtalif al-Hadeeth)04-31)* is by Ibn Qudaamah, and at-Tahaawee has the work *((Mushkil al-Athaar)04-34)*, and Imaam Shaafa'ee has *((Mukhtalif al-Hadeeth)04-25)*. All these book gather together numerous hadeeth narrations that seem to contradict each other, and then explain according to the principles of the Sharee'ah and evidence why they in fact do not. However, they often wrongly try to reconcile between two hadeeth narrations which are weak and not accepted, and it is necessary that we leave both of those unauthentic narrations, and adhere to what is judged to be authentic.

*Benefit:* Imaam Muslim mentions in the introduction to his "Saheeh" collection that in presenting the hadeeth it contains, he has first put forth that which is most authentic and after this those authentic narrations of a slightly lower level. Yet this is not something he applied uniformly within the collection.

*Benefit:* From those hadeeth scholars who have compiled works about those narrators with the name 'Ataa is at-Tabaraanee.

*Benefit:* The best book written about those scholars from whom the scholars of the six principal hadeeth collections narrated hadeeth from- meaning so and so narrated from so-and-so- is the book of Ibn Asaakir *((Mashaaykh)05-28)*

*Benefit:* I came across a book by an evildoing Raafidhee, Saaleh al-Wardaanee, in which he ridicules and mocks Sheikh Ibn Baaz. This book is evidence that they were destroyed by his collected rulings and statements, because they were not able to respond with any knowledge-based refutations, only empty mocking. So this is an clear expression of their overwhelming spite and hatefulness.

*Benefit:* The book of Abu Haamed *((Darasatun wa Naqd)11-32)* is very beneficial. He is one of the students of al-Albaanee, named 'Abdur-Rahman ad-Dimashqee.

*Benefit:* The book *((Ajweebah Abee Mas'ood)04-35),* written in response to the specific criticism of some of the narrations of Saheeh Muslim by his own Sheikh ad-Darqutnee, is a response written with the highest degree of justice and fairness.

*Benefit:* The book *((Radd 'Alaa al-Jahmeeyah)11-10)* is attributed to Imaam Ahmad. I do not know that it has been affirmed to have authentically been authored by him.

*Benefit:* The book 'as-Sifaat' by Darqutnee, cannot be authentically attributed to him. There are other works which are more than sufficient for you such as *((as-Sunnah)06-26)* by al-Khilaal, the work of *((Lalaka'ee)06-29)*, *((at-Tawheed)06-36)* by Ibn Khusaymah, and *((al-'Asmaa wa as-Sifaat)06-35)* by al-Bayhaqee.

*Benefit:* The work *((Lisaan al-Mizaan)05-20)* does remove the need for *((Mizaan al-'Itidaal)05-19)* because even though Ibn Hajr added other additional narrators and criticized adh-Dhahabee's assessment of certain narrators, he removed from his work those narrators from the six principal hadeeth collections whom adh-Dhahabee discussed which he had already examined within his other work *((Tadheeb at-Tadheeb)05-18).*

*Benefit:* The book [[al-Aghaanee]] by Abee al-Farj al-Asbahaanee contains a defense of the sect of the Shee'ah; therefore do not use or rely up it.

*Benefit:* The historian Muhammd al-Akwaa' has a verification of the book *((Qurrat al-Ayyun fee Akhbaar al-Yemeen)12-20)* which is a good historical verification.

*[FROM THE EXPEDITIONS OF SHEIKH MUQBIL IBN HAADEE AL-WAADI'EE WHEN CALLING TO ALLAAH, PAGES 121-123]*

# (42)

QUESTION: AS FOR THOSE WHO WERE PREVIOUSLY CONSIDERED TO BE UPON THE CORRECT METHODOLOGY AND THEN DEVIATED FROM IT, IS IT PERMISSIBLE FOR US TO LISTEN TO THEIR TAPES OR TO READ THEIR BOOKS WHICH THEY WROTE IN THE PAST, AND SIMILARLY THEIR RECORDED LECTURES?

nswer: I do not advise reading their books or listening to their audio lectures. And I was once impressed by a tremendous statement from Sheikh al-Islaam Ibn Taymeeyah, may Allaah have mercy upon him. He said related to this issue, "If Allaah had not brought forth Imaam al-Bukhaaree or Imaam Muslim, still no harm would have reached this religion of His. Allaah, the Most Glorified and the Most Exalted, has certainly preserved and protected this religion. Allaah the Exalted says: ◈*Verily It is We Who have sent down the Dhikr and surely, We will guard it (from corruption*◈-(*Surah Hijr:*9) So I advise you to stay far away from their books, audio tapes, and their lectures where they stand as callers. They themselves are in need of being invited and called to the truth, and in need of returning back to the Book of Allaah and to the Sunnah of Allaah's Messenger, may Allaah's praise and salutations be upon him. They themselves need to repent to Allaah, the Most Glorified and the Most Exalted, from that which appeared from specific individuals from among them during the events of the Gulf War as well as concerning other matters.

*[FROM 'EXCELLENT RESPONSES TO QUESTIONS FROM THOSE PRESENT AND THOSE ABSENT': PAGE 209]*

# (43)

QUESTION: WE OBSERVE THAT SOME OF THOSE WHO AFFILIATE THEMSELVES WITH THE METHODOLOGY OF THE FIRST THREE GENERATIONS CHOOSE TO OCCUPY THEMSELVES WITH CRITICISM AND WARNING FROM THE ASTRAY GROUPS AND SECTS, WHILE NEGLECTING THE SEEKING OF KNOWLEDGE; WHEREAS OTHERS WHO CLAIM THE SAME METHODOLOGY DO GIVE PRIORITY TO SEEKING KNOWLEDGE YET TURN AWAY FROM THE MATTER OF WARNINGS AND CRITICISMS. IT HAS REACHED THE STATE WHERE THOSE OF THE SECOND GROUP SAY, "CERTAINLY, CRITICIZING IS NOT FROM THE METHODOLOGY OF THE PEOPLE OF THE SUNNAH AT ALL." SO WHAT IS CORRECT IN THIS ISSUE?

nswer: As for those who occupy themselves solely with critically examining the mistakes of others and warning from them- they can be considered disproportionate in their affairs of seeking knowledge, as found in the answers to the questions of our brothers from the Emirates, as well as their being excessive in focusing on the realm of criticism. What is seen when one considers the lives of our previous scholars? If we look at the biography of Ibn Abee Haatim, we find that he was a tremendous memorizer; indeed he was even given the title of Sheikh al-Islaam. The same case can be seen with Imaam al-Bukhaaree, Imaam Ahmad Ibn Hanbal, Yahya Ibn Ma'een, Yahya Ibn Sa'ed al-Qahtaan, Abu Haatim, Abu Zura'ah, ad-Darqutnee, Ibn Hibaan, and Haakim. They wrote many beneficial books, such as in the subject of the explanations of the Qur'aan,as well as works in the various hadeeth sciences. They produced beneficial works and preserved for us the Sunnah of the Messenger of Allaah, may Allaah's praise and salutations be upon him and his household.

But in addition they also produced beneficial books related to criticism and commendation of individuals in the religion. Therefore it is necessary that we join between the first focus and priority and the second, as otherwise an individual will be deficient from one aspect, as well as being excessive from another.

I ask you, according to what criterion will we assess the state of individuals if we are ignorant of beneficial knowledge? Will we simply judge them by our desires or by following what has been said by sheikh so and so? Such that if Sheikh so-and-so recants a position we also recant it, and if he holds a position regarding a number of individuals then we also hold it. Therefore it can be seen that it is necessary that we combine the first matter and the second.

As for the second group which was mentioned, those who only give attention to knowledge without raising their heads towards commending or criticizing anyone, then in my view, of the two groups overall they are in a better state than the first group. The first group is attempting to enter into or concern themselves with an area which is not within their present ability to confront personally. Yet despite this fact, it is clear that this second group has itself torn down or subverted an important aspect of Islaam. Indeed, that work of our brother Bakr Ibn 'Abdullah Abu Zayd [[*Categorizing the People between Doubt and Certainty*]] in this subject should be considered the worst book from those which he wrote. On the other hand, many of his works, all praise is due to Allaah, are from the best of those available, may Allaah reward him with good.

But as for the destruction of the role or position of criticizing and commending in the religion, then know that Allaah the Most Glorified and Most Exalted has Himself has said in His Noble Book, *And do not obey every worthless habitual swearer and scorner, going about with malicious gossip - A preventer of good, transgressing and sinful, Cruel, moreover, and an illegitimate pretender.*-(Surah al-Qalam: 10-13) And He said, *Perish the two hands of Abu Lahab and perish he! His wealth and his children will not benefit him! He will be burnt in a Fire of blazing flames! And his wife too, who carries wood. Around her neck is a twisted rope of fiber.*-(Surah al-Masad: 1-5). Allaah, the Most Perfect and the Most High, has criticized Abu Lahab and also criticized his wife. Likewise Musa, when he intended to strike the one with him from the previous incident of killing, said to him. *Indeed, you are an evident, persistent deviator.* These are all evidence of the permissibility of legitimate criticism of someone.

The Prophet, may Allaah's praise and salutations be upon him and his household, said regarding a man who came to sit with him, *{What an evil man of the tribe he is.}* But when that man entered, he sat with him and spoke with him nicely. 'Aishah then asked why he did that after having criticized him, and he replied, *{The worst people, in the sight of Allaah are those whom the people abandon to save themselves from their foul language.}*. This is narrated in both Saheeh al-Bukhaaree and Saheeh Muslim on the authority of 'Aishah.

It is also narrated in Saheeh al-Bukhaaree from the hadeeth of 'Aishah, that one of the women from the household of Abu Sufyan said, *"Abu Sufyaan is a man who is miserly, not giving us what is sufficient."* The Prophet, may Allaah's praise and salutations be upon him and his household, remained silent regarding her criticism of Abu Sufyan. Moreover, in another instance the Prophet, may Allaah's praise and salutations be upon him and his household, asked, *{Who is your chief, oh Banu Salaamah?" They replied al-Jad Ibn Qays, yet we see him to be a miser."* So the Prophet, may Allaah's praise and salutations be upon him and his household, said, "So which disease is worse than miserliness? Rather, your chief is 'Amr Ibn al-Jamooh."}* [1]. And the Prophet, may Allaah's praise and salutations be upon him and his household, said to Mu'adh Ibn Jabal, *{Are you a trial for the people, oh Mu'adh?!}* [2]. And he said to Abu Dhar, *{Indeed you are a man who has some aspects of those days of ignorance before Islaam still within him.}*-(Saheeh al-Bukhaaree: 30, 6050, Saheeh Muslim: 1661). And he said to some of the women of his household, *{Indeed, you are like some of the evil women who tempted Prophet Yusuf.}*-(Saheeh al-Bukhaaree: 664 & other narrations, Saheeh Muslim: 418). This was narrated by Imaam al-Bukhaaree in his Saheeh. And the Prophet, may Allaah's praise and salutations be upon him and his household, said,

---

[1]    Narrated in al-Adab al-Mufrad: 296/ & al-Mustadrak alaa Saheehayn: 4953/ -on the authority of Ab Hurairah. It was declared authentic by Sheikh al-Albaanee in Saheeh al-Adab al-Mufrad: 296.

[2]    Narrated in Saheeh al-Bukhaaree: 705, 6106/ Saheeh Muslim: 465/ Sunan Abu Dawud: 790/ Sunan an-Nasaa'ee: 832, 836, 985, 998/ & Musnad Imaam Ahmad: 13778, 13895: -on the authority of Jaabir Ibn 'Abdullah. It was declared authentic by Sheikh al-Albaanee in Irwa' al-Ghaleel: 295, Mishkaat al-Masaabeh: 833, Saheeh al-Jaame'a as-Sagheer: 7966. Sheikh Muqbil declared it authentic in al-Jaame'a al-Saheeh: 240, 1026, 3628, 3630.

*{I do not believe that so and so and so and so understands anything at all from our religion.}*-(Saheeh al-Bukhaaree: 6068) Laith Ibn Sa'd explained this as referring to two of the hypocrites who did not truly embrace Islaam.

And the Prophet, may Allaah's praise and salutations be upon him and his household, said to Hamal Ibn Maalik Ibn an-Naabighah in judgment when it occurred that a woman from his people struck another woman with something which caused the other woman to abort the unborn child she was carrying, *{"They should be given a male or a female slave in compensation." So Hamal Ibn Maalik Ibn an-Naabighah said, "Oh Messenger of Allaah, why should we pay for that which has never eaten nor drunk anything, nor was even born. One such as this should not be considered." So the Prophet, may Allaah's praise and salutations be upon him and his household, said, "This one is from the brothers of the magicians"}* -(Saheeh al-Bukhaaree: 5758, 5760, Saheeh Muslim: 1681), due to his arguing using rhymed poetry.

And the Prophet, may Allaah's praise and salutations be upon him and his household, said, *{The extremists are destroyed, The extremists are destroyed, The extremists are destroyed.}* -(Saheeh Muslim: 2670, Sunan Abu Dawud: 4608). And he said regarding the sect of the Khawaarij, *{Indeed, they are the dogs of the Hellfire.}* [3]. He also said, *{Indeed, they will pass through the religion the way an arrow passes through the animal that was shot at.}* -(Saheeh al-Bukhaaree: 3344).

Therefore the one who is deficient in implementing criticism and commendation in the religion, is then deficient in implementing an aspect of the Sunnah. If criticism and commendation are not implemented then everyone speaks claiming to be a *"caller to Allaah"* or an *"esteemed scholar,"* such as is seen in the speech of 'Alee at-Tantaawee, or the

[3]   Narrated in Sunan Ibn Maajah: 173/ & Musnad Imaam Ahmad: 18651, 18923: -on the authority of Ibn Abee 'Awf. It was declared authentic by Sheikh al-Albaanee in Dhelaal al-Jannah: 905. Sheikh Muqbil declared it authentic in al-Jaame'a al-Saheeh: 254, 645, 2349, 3305, 3954.

speech of Mahmood as-Sawaaf, or the speech of Muhammad al-Ghazaalee, or the speech of Hassan at-Turaabee, or the speech of as-Sharaawee, or the speech of the different Shee'ah and Rawaafidh, or such as the speech of the Sufee -Hasan Saqqaaf.

Therefore I say no one knowingly turns away from understanding of this branch of knowledge except an individual who is ignorant, or an individual with a spiteful heart, or an individual who comes to know that he has himself been criticized, so he then has an aversion to criticism and commendation in the religion due to the fact that he learns that he has been publicly criticized. Yet Allaah rejects anything other than what brings victory to His religion and makes supreme His word, and brings forth the truth. The people of the Sunnah have now given priority to criticism and commendation for the sake of the religion, while before it was as if some of them were sleeping, so Allaah brought forth those people those who would awaken them. Before, some of them didn't used to speak extensively in matters of commendation and criticism, as if this was something specific to the period of Imaam al-Bukhaaree and Muslim.

But I say clearly, shouldn't we criticize the one in this age who says, [Popular Democracy is compatible with Islaam.]? In reality, is not the correct way that we criticize the one who makes such a false claim and strive to explain to the people that the one who makes this claim is a deceiver from the many deceivers? Shouldn't we criticize those individuals who speak against and attack the scholars of the Muslims? Additionally, how could we, as we do, criticize our own esteemed scholars in some knowledge-based issues, yet consider it proper to remain silent about these more significant matters?!?

Therefore it is necessary that we join between these two matters, and focus both on seeking knowledge as well as criticism and warning against those who have opposed the truth. When we read the biographies of the Companions and read the biographies of the Successors to the Companions as well as those of the generation that followed them –the Successors of those Successors- we find that they often made statements that reflected this. Where do we stand when we hear the statements of Imaam ad-Dhahabee, "*Zatn, who is Zatn? He is only is a deceiver from among the deceivers, claiming that he is a Companion six hundred years after the year of the Hijra!*" Or when we hear the likes of the statements of Imaam as-Shaafa'ee who said, "*Narrating on Haram Ibn 'Uthmaan is itself haraam (forbidden).*" Or another statement from Imaam as-Shaafa'ee, "*The one who narrates on al-Bayaadhee (meaning a person of whiteness), may Allaah make his eyes white with blindness.*" Where do we stand when we hear such statements? Do we say that Imaam as-Shaafa'ee is from those who are harsh and unnecessarily severe, someone who was wrong in speaking against the Muslims or in speaking about those scholars?

We challenge you to prove with evidence that we have falsely spoken against any of the scholars, or against those advocating popular Democracy, or those who speak from this personal opinion or that personal opinion, or those who affirm the various mandates and resolutions of the United Nations or that of the Council of Nations, or those who say, [This age is not one of saying "so and so informed me" and "so and so narrated to me," or of stating that this narration is authentic or this one is weak.] And we respond to this last by saying, indeed this is certainly the age for this, as many hadeeth narrations presently circulating among the people are either weak or fabricated. I conclude what I have said with what was mentioned by al-Haafidh as-Sooree, may Allaah have mercy upon him, who said:

> *Say to the one who opposes narrations of hadeeth and*
>> *comes forth blaming the people of hadeeth and those who adhere to them,*

*Do you say this to me based upon knowledge, my son,*

> *or does it come from ignorance, as ignorance is the character of a fool.*

*Do you blame those who strive to preserve the religion?*

> *from falsehoods, lies, and distortions,*

*and find fault with their statements while what they narrate*

> *is referred to by every true scholar and those with understanding of the religion?*

And I do not intend by this that the one upon the Sunnah should unnecessarily occupy his time with this. Rather, one should occupy some of his time with clarifying the mistakes of the various sects and groups, and a good portion of his time for easy breathing and necessary rest, and also some time for eating and drinking, and so on. Indeed, what I intend is that one be as has been said:

*A man stands with his feet firmly upon the earth,*

> *but indeed the highest of his goals is in the stars.*

Some of our brothers in Islaam have written to me and said, [Do not preoccupy yourself with these matters.] They incorrectly believe that I am preoccupied with these matters, while in fact, all praise is due to Allaah, I am not. My efforts of composition and writing have their own time, as do my classes given in order to teach the people, and matters of criticism and commendation of individuals for the sake of the religion also has its place and time. Ibn Jawzee confronted the people of his time because of their using and narrating weak or fabricated hadeeth, and this practice is similarly present today. Likewise, others besides him from the scholars of the first generations confronted the people of their ages regarding the use of weak or fabricated narrations, and similarly people who engage in this are undoubtedly present today. Yet, all praise is due to Allaah, the knowledge of the Sunnah has spread tremendously, such that even the "Bankrupt Brotherhood" (the Muslim Brotherhood organization) is now teaching the science of hadeeth terminology! However as is said:

> *They praise the efforts of the guard, yet he acts only for the sake of trying,*
>
> > *to retain in those young men already among them- so that they do not run away.*

Look at 'Abdullah Sa'tar from their group who has taken up the book *((Sharh at-Tahaweeyah)06-09)* and it now teaching it. Oh 'Abdullah Sa'tar, you have certainly undertaken a difficult ascent! So what happened is that on the first night of those classes there was a large group of people attending, and the second night there were less, and on the third night even less. Thereafter, there were perhaps only seven people present, and then later maybe three.

Because in terms of knowledge, he actually doesn't have a firm grasp of matters except to know that such and such was said in the newspaper "al-Hayaat," and that such and such was mentioned by the "London Broadcast," and that such and such paper mentioned this or that. Therefore it is clear through their efforts that what they desire is only that their youth remain with them and not abandon them. So they announce: "We are teaching the issues of belief!" "We are teaching hadeeth terminology!" and so forth and so on. However we see regarding them, as it is said, "Eventually Haleemah just returned from her previous ways." So when they see that this way neither really profited them and their objectives, they will return once again to their way of lies and deception.

*[FROM 'ADVICES & CLARIFICATIONS': PAGES 111- 117]*

# (44)

QUESTION: SOME PEOPLE ACCUSE THE PEOPLE OF THE SUNNAH OF BEING HARSH. HOW SHOULD WE RESPOND TO THEM?

nswer: In truth we know our ownselves better than others know us. So the one who would accuse us of being those who have fallen short, and lax in what is necessary, then I bear witness to Allaah that He is the truthful! Otherwise we say that we wish to be of those who are moderate, neither falling short nor going to any extremes. I advise our brother to read the book *((Qaraa' Alasat fe Nafee al-Ghuluu wa at-Tatraf wa al-Ashadhudh 'An Ahl-Sunnah)11-14)* until he understands the reality of this matter. So where is the required enjoining what is right and the forbidding what is wrong? Where is the self-sacrifice among us, where is the diligence in teaching others? In fact, we are those who have fallen short in what is required in this area, so I ask Allaah to forgive us, and accept our repentance. However, those who adhere to innovations in the religion contradict themselves regarding their claims about the people of the Sunnah. Sometimes they say, [They are extremists who are harsh!] and other times they say, [They just sit in their masjids reciting this and narrating that, and they have abandoned calling to Allaah and have left truly striving in the path of Allaah!] So in reality, the people of innovation are self-contradictory in their various conflicting claims about the people of the Sunnah.

*[FROM 'BRIDLING THE RESISTANT ONE': PAGE 326]*

# (45)

QUESTION: WHAT IS THE DIFFERENCE
BETWEEN A STATEMENT OF CRITICISM
AND GIVING ADVICE?

nswer: The difference between a statement of criticism and the giving of advice is that in relation to advice it is possible that it be given privately, only between the one giving the advice and the one being advised. As Allaah says, *And speak to him mildly, perhaps he may accept admonition or fear Allaah.*-(Surah Taha:44) But as for a statement of criticism, most likely it is something written in books, or mentioned in public gatherings. Our scholars from the early centuries, may Allaah have mercy upon all of them, combined both of these matters. Imaam adh-Dhahabee, may Allaah have mercy upon him said, "*Ratan, and who is this Rattan? A lying deceiver from among the lying deceivers who falsely claims to be a Companion six hundred years after their period.*" And Imaam Sha'fee- may Allaah have mercy upon him said, "*Narrating on Haraam Ibn 'Uthma'n is haraam (meaning forbidden)*," and he also said, "*As for the one who narrated from al-Badhaee may Allaah whiten his eyes (as in blindness).*". In relation to the false hadeeth narration from Suwayd Ibn Saeed: [The one who loved passionately but remained chaste, and held back from his desires, dies the death of a martyr... ]Yahya Ibn Ma'een said: "*If only I had a horse and a spear with which to fight against this man Suwayd...*" And it was requested from Shu'bah that he stop criticizing 'Abaan Ibn Abee Aeeash, as he 'Abaan- was an excellent individual occupied with worship and having little concern for worldly matters, but he was of those who confused matters when narrating hadeeth. So he initially said, "*I will consider this*". But later he replied to the one who gave him this advice by saying, "*This is related to the religion, and as such there is no possible course for me to follow except that I continue speak regarding the condition of 'Abaan Ibn Abee Aeeash.*" And Abu Haneefah, may Allaah have mercy upon him, spoke regarding Jaabir Ibn Yazeed al-Jaafee, "*I have not seen a greater liar than him.*" And Sha'bee may Allaah have mercy upon him, declared al-Harith Ibn 'Abdullah al-

Hamdanee a liar. And we have mentioned some aspect of this issue in the introduction to the work *(Makhraj min al-Fitnah)11-21)* as found in the second and third editions, as well as the introduction to *(Rudood Ahlul-Ilm Ala At-Taa'neen fee Hadeeth As-Sahr wa Bayan B'ued Muhammad Rasheed Ridha 'An As-Salafeeyah)11-25)*. And all praise is due to Allaah, both of these books are printed.

*[FROM 'A DEFENDING MISSION FROM AUDIO LECTURES UPON THE PEOPLE OF IGNORANCE & SOPHISTRY': VOL 1, PAGE 71 ]*

# (46)

QUESTION: IS IT TRUE THAT LEARNING TO RECITE WITH TAJWEED IS OBLIGATORY UPON EVERY MUSLIM? THE AUTHOR OF THE BOOK "THE STUDY OF TAJWEED" STATES, "IT IS OBLIGATORY" AND HE DERIVES THIS FROM THE STATEMENT OF ALLAAH THE EXALTED, ﴾RECITE THE QUR'AAN PROPERLY﴿

nswer: What is correct in this issue is that reciting with tajweed is not obligatory. The verse *Recite the Qur'aan properly*-(Surah al-Muzammmil: 4) means to recite clearly and make the Qur'aan clearly heard, not mumbled and jumbled, mixing up the different letters together. As for the statement of al-Jazaree:

*Reciting with tajweed is an obligatory injunction,*

*the one who recites the Qur'aan without it is a sinner.*

*Because he has lowered the station of his High Lord*

*And so along with us that is what he has become.*

Then this is not correct. Rather it is found in the two well-known "Saheeh" collection of al-Bukhaaree and Muslim that 'Aishah, may Allaah be pleased with her said, that the Messenger of Allaah, may Allaah's praise and salutations be upon him, said, *{The proficient reciter of the Qur'aan is associated with the noble and the upright, recording angels, and the one who makes mistakes and finds it difficult for him will have a double reward}* -(Saheeh al-Bukhaaree: 4937, Saheeh Muslim: 798).

So this is in relation to the obligation reciting it correctly; but as for the matter of beautifying it with one's voice then this is only a matter which is desired and recommended. It is found in the 'Sunan' collections of hadeeth the narration of al-Baraa' Ibn 'Aazib, may Allaah be pleased with him, where he said that the Messenger of Allaah, may Allaah's praise and salutations be upon him, said, *{Beautify the Qur'aan with your voices.}* [1]. And as is found on authority of Sa'eed Ibn Abee Waqaas, may Allaah be pleased with him, the Messenger of Allaah, may Allaah's praise and salutations be upon him, said, *{The one who does not strive to beautify the Qur'aan with his voice, is not from among us.}* -(Saheeh al-Bukhaaree:

---

[1] Narrated in Sunan Abu Dawud: 1468/ & other collections: -on the authority of Baraa' Ibn 'Aazab. It was declared authentic by Sheikh al-Albaanee in Silsilat al-Hadeeth as-Saheehah: 771 and within other works. Sheikh Muqbil declared it authentic in al-Jaame'a al-Saheeh: 347, 1019, 3845, 3846, 4668.

7527). Meaning the one who does not try to use his voice to recite the Qur'aan in a pleasing way, then he is not from us.

It is also found in the two well-known "Saheeh" collection of al-Bukhaaree and Muslim from Abu Hurairah, may Allaah be pleased with him, that the Messenger of Allaah, may Allaah's praise and salutations be upon him, *{Allah never listens to anything as much He listens to the Prophet reciting Qur'aan in a pleasant sweet sounding voice.}*- (Saheeh al-Bukhaaree: 5024, 7482, 7544, Saheeh Muslim: 792) Therefore reciting while beautifying one's voice is a recommended matter as indicated by the principles of Arabic language. One of those who takes an extreme position regarding tajweed used to teach us, and he would say, "The Arabs even used the rules of tajweed in their poetry," Then he would recite the line of poetry:

*Hold your tears from remembering your beloved and your home...*

And he said this verse of poetry with Qalqala on the Arabic letter baa, and joining the tanween and the Arabic letter waw of the following word together.[2] So it was said to him in criticism, "*Oh Sheikh, where is the chain of narration to Amr' al-Qays, (the poet of the above lines) which shows that he read this poetry as you have read it?!?*" Similarly, Haafidh Ibn Qayyim, mentioned in *((Ighathatul al-Lahfaan)12-05)* that this is considered from being among the traps of Shaytaan-unbalanced over-stringent focus upon reciting according to the rules of tajweed. He said, "*Some of the reciters will occupy a student of knowledge learning to recite for forty days over his recitation of Surat al-Faatihah alone.*" And he also said, "*Some of them will be so thoroughly obsessed with trying to recite in this way that he recites it until it is as though he were vomiting; his veins become swollen, and his face reddens until it looks like he is about to vomit.*"

---

[2]     This is a reference to some of the specific guidelines of tajweed he used when reciting this poetry

But the people should stand between both extremism and neglect. From among the people there is the one who does not give any concern to beautifying his voice when reciting the Qur'aan, and from among the people there are those who go to extreme lengths for the sake of beautification. And if you heard such a one reciting and you are far away from him, you could not be sure whether he was reciting the Qur'aan and or simply singing.

Yet the first generations of believers, may Allaah be pleased with them all, criticized this over-stringent focus on beautification of recitation. Some of them criticized Hamzah (one of the early Qur'aan reciters) regarding some of his recitation, such that some of our predecessors, may Allaah the Most High, have mercy upon them, stated, "*The method of recitation of Hamza is an innovation in the religion,*" as is mentioned in the work *((Mizaan al-'Itidaal)05-19)*. So over-stringent focus regarding beautification through tajweed is something blameworthy, just as a failure to give due consideration to reciting according to the guidelines of tajweed is considered neglectfulness in the religion. Therefore is proper that you sit and learn from one who will teach you the guidelines of tajweed and benefit from him, but as for considering it obligatory, then no, this is incorrect.

Rather this matter is as has been mentioned by ash-Shawkaanee, may Allaah have mercy upon him, in the biography of Muhammad Ibn Ibraaheem al-Wazeer, may Allaah have mercy upon him, as found in the book *((al-Badr al-Talaa')05-29)*. He stated, "*Some of the people overly praise in their writings an area from amongst the different areas of knowledge, because of their delighting in it, and they make it the embodiment of excellence in knowledge. Thereafter later scholars read their words, and come to consider that this matter is from the obligatory matters of Sharee'ah knowledge, and that is required to study it.*"

So you should benefit from the one who knows how to recite according to the guidelines of tajweed, and be diligent and learning how to recite with tajweed, and hold fast to learning the Arabic language. The Qur'aan was revealed in the Arabic language, it did not come in a foreign language, or in the language of the people of Damaaj, or of 'Aden, or Hadhramaut, or America, such that you would want to recite the Qur'aan and that language. No, rather the Qur'aan is to be recited in the Arabic language just as it was revealed. This is what is proper. And some of the people say, [But the specific guidelines of tajweed are taken with chains of narration to their original reciters, and original reciters back to the Prophet, may Allaah's praise and salutations be upon him.] Then you should say to them, "*Where within these chains of narration are found the specific rules regarding elongation the letter 'aleef' here, with a single period of elongation, and in some places to periods of elongation, while in other places it is four or six.??*"

Yes it is true that it is affirmed on the Prophet, may Allaah's praise and salutations be upon him and his household, that he used to recite the letter 'aleef' with elongation in some places, therefore you should recite and beautify your recitation as Allaah has commanded you. But some of the people go to extremes, they make al-ikhfaa' (which is a concealing of the sound of letter accompanied by with a nasal sound to idgham (meaning here the full merging of a specific type of the letter into the letter that follows it when suitable), and they may extend the pronunciation of a word until it practically has been wrongly merged with that which follows it. Yet Allaah says, ❧*Say (Oh Muhammad): "Oh people of the Scripture (Jews and Christians)! Do not exceed the limits in your religion*❧- (Surah An-Nisa': 171)  So what is proper for us is that we engage in reciting, and that we gauge correctness according to the recitation of the Messenger of Allaah, may Allaah's praise and salutations be upon him and his household, and according to the recitation of the Companions, may Allaah be pleased with them all, and the recitation of the first generations in general, may Allaah be pleased with them all. There is a significant distinction between an individual improperly mumbling or jumbling together his recitation of the Qur'aan, and a different individual who recites clearly and beautifully. As a person is affected by the one who recites clearly and beautifully.

Indeed, as is mentioned in the 'Saheeh' collection of al-Bukhaaree, a man came to Ibn Mas'ood, may Allaah be pleased with him, and said, "*I recited the shorter Mufassal surahs at night in one rak'ah.*" Ibn Mas'ud said, "*This recitation is too quick, like the recitation of poetry.*" So the matter is undertaken in a middle way. And this verse is to be considered a ruling with ❧*Recite the Qur'aan properly*❧-(Surah al-Muzzammel:4) meaning, recite clearly and distinctly. Make sure that each letter and each word is distinct. And some of the imaams of prayer who lead the people in prayer, it is seen that there is no way that he could have recited the opening supplication in his prayer. He says, "*Allaahu Akbar,*" and then immediately he begins reciting al-Fatiha, and another Surah after it, without any break. This is playing with the religion, and certainly the best guidance is the guidance of Muhammad, may Allaah's praise and salutations be upon him and his household, in how he recited during the ritual prayer, as well as in the remaining matters of ritual worship, the guidance of every day affairs, as well as in our essential beliefs.

*[FROM 'BRIDLING THE RESISTANT ONE', PAGE 434]*

# (47)

QUESTION: WHAT IS THE CORRECT WAY TO MEMORIZE THE QUR'AAN AND AHADEETH?

nswer: In regard to the memorization of the Qur'aan, then the people differ. Among people, one person may be able to memorize an entire page, and someone may be able to memorize several pages, and from them someone may only be able to memorize half a page or less. So everyone proceeds according to his ability and capacity. From those matters which aid and strengthen you in memorizing the Qur'aan is repetition and continual review, as well as standing in prayer in night, for the one who has the ability to stand at night. As Allaah, glorified be He, the Most High, said, ❦ *Verily, the rising by night for Tahajjud prayer is very hard and most potent and good for governing the soul*❧-(Surah al-Muzzammel:6) and He said: ❦*And in some parts of the night also offer the salaat with it (i.e. recite the Qur'aan in the prayer), as an additional prayer for you*❧-(Surah al-Isra'a:79)

Also, take from the scholars in this area and memorize at their hands. If this is not possible for you then I advise you to obtain cassette tapes of precise narrators who recite with correct recitation. Not those reciters who stretch their recitation excessively as is done by such as the famous reciter 'Abdul-Baasset. No, only the one who recites in a moderate and balanced way, and not from those who do so in a manner that was hated by some of the first generations of Muslims. As for the memorization of hadeeth narrations then this is somewhat easier. If you can proceed without memorizing the chains of narration, then it may be possible to memorize a single hadeeth in one, two or perhaps three days. Then you should act upon and implement this hadeeth, as this will help the hadeeth become firmly rooted in your memory. Afterwords, be consistent to reviewing it with some of your brothers, as well as frequently repeating and reviewing it in general.

*[FROM 'EXCELLENT RESPONSES TO QUESTIONS FROM THOSE PRESENT AND THOSE ABSENT': PAGE 157]*

# (48)

QUESTION: WHAT ARE THE CAUSES
THAT ASSIST THE STUDENT OF
KNOWLEDGE IN MEMORIZATION, MAY
ALLAAH BLESS YOU WITH GOOD?

nswer: From the greatest of matters which assist a student of knowledge in memorizing are first: fearing Allaah, the Most Glorified and the Most Exalted as Allaah says, *So have fear of Allaah; and Allaah will instruct you.*-(Surah al-Baqarah:282) and He said, *Oh you who believe! If you obey and fear Allaah, He will grant you a criterion to judge between right and wrong*-(Surah al-Anfaal:29) and He said, *Oh you who believe fear Allaah, and believe too in His Messenger, He will give you a double portion of His Mercy, and He will give you a light by which you shall walk straight*-(Surah al-Haadeed: 28). After this, having purity of intention in your acquiring knowledge for Allaah, the Most High and the Most Exalted's sake alone; Allaah, the Most Glorified and the Most Exalted says, *Surely, the religion i.e. the worship and the obedience is for Allaah only*-(Surah az-Zumar:3). Indeed, we have seen that a person who has purity of intention will prevail over someone who possesses more knowledge than him. Then after this is a good deal of review and repetition, as this strengthens and assists memorization.

Also, distance yourself from problems; for an individual, if is he is overburdened with problems, then he is not able to memorize and if he does manage to memorize, he will often forget what was memorized. The matters above are the more abstract matters. Now as for more practical matters that will also assist you in memorization, from them is: eating foods that are considered of a sweet nature, such as dates, raisins, and honey, as well foods considered hot or spicy, such as black pepper and ginger- but do not consume too much of these two. If you have used them excessively then they may cause you to be depressed. Then after this fling far from you anxiety and whispered doubts and be strict in mastering the issues you are studying. Likewise from such beneficial foods is yogurt, as it strengthens one's efforts of memorization, with the condition that one not use it too much. If you use it excessively, perhaps you will become anxious and weaken your memorization. From the matters which lead to a weakening of your memorization are being preoccupied with your body, whether this is related to pursuing sexual relations or some other related matter. These matters weaken an individual, and may strip from him and what information or knowledge he possesses. Additionally, if you have memorized the Qur'aan, from those matter which will assist you in preserving that memorization is reciting while standing in the night prayer. ❖ *Verily, the rising by night (for Tahajjud prayer) is very hard and most potent and good for governing (the soul), and most suitable for (understanding) the Word (of Allaah).* ❖-(Surah Muzammil: 6). This assists an individual in retaining that which he has memorized.

*[FROM 'THE FINAL TRAVELS OF THE IMAAM OF THE ARAB PENINSULA' BY UMM SALAMAH AS-SALAFEEYAH, PAGE 281]*

# (49)

QUESTION: CAN WE TAKE FROM THE BOOK VERIFICATIONS OF SHU'AYB AL-ARNOUT AND HIS BROTHER?

nswer: We benefit from the book verifications of these two, and there are not many remarks to be made in regard to them. So benefit from their efforts in verification of books. In most cases they have benefitted from the general verifications and hadeeth source verifications of Sheikh Naasirudden al-Albaanee, may Allaah the Exalted preserve him. And what I advise each of my brothers in Islaam is to strive to reach an assessment of authenticity of narrations yourself, and to be of those who have high goals and aspirations -as was said by the poet:

*A man stands with his feet firmly upon the earth,*

    *but indeed the highest of his goals is in the stars.*

[FROM 'ANSWERING THE QUESTIONER REGARDING THE MOST IMPORTANT ISSUES': PAGE 564]

# (50)

QUESTION: ALONG WITH THE MANY PEOPLE WHO VERIFY THE BOOKS FROM OUR RIGHTEOUS PREDECESSORS IN THIS AGE, THERE ARE SOME VERIFIERS WHO INITIALLY BROUGHT FORTH BOOKS IN WHICH ARE FOUND BENEFICIAL POINTS REGARDING GENERAL KNOWLEDGE AND CORRECT BELIEF. THEN AFTER THEY BECAME WELL KNOWN AMONG THE RANKS OF YOUTH, THEY BEGAN TO BRING FORTH STRANGE STATEMENTS AND INCONSISTENCIES. HOW CAN THE YOUTH DEAL WITH THIS SITUATION, WHEN THERE IS LITTLE OR NO WARNING FROM THE SCHOLARS REGARDING THESE SHORTCOMINGS? FROM THESE VERIFIERS, AS AN EXAMPLE, IS THE SHEIKH 'ABDUL-QAADIR AL-ARNAA'OUT AND HIS VERIFICATION OF 'AQAAWEL AT-THIQAAT' OF KAREMEE. WE BENEFIT FROM HIS INTRODUCTION IN RELATION TO ISSUES OF CORRECT BELIEF AND HIS REFUTATION THE DISTORTION OF THE SOURCE TEXTS BY ASHA'REE SECT. HOWEVER IN CONTRAST TO THIS, IN HIS COMMENTS IN 'SAHEEH IBN HIBBAAN', HE BRINGS FORTH SIMILAR DISTORTIONS OF THEM OF SOME ATTRIBUTES OF ALLAAH AND LEGITIMIZES THIS. SO WE HOPE FOR A WARNING FROM THESE ERRORS, AND THAT YOU CLARIFY FOR US THE CONDITION AND LEVEL OF SOME OF THE AUTHORS AND VERIFIERS IN OUR TIME.

nswer: It is an obligation upon the brother to write to him and advise him of this issue. Likewise, in truth, the brother Shu'ayb al-Arnaa'out has produced valuable books for the students of knowledge; so based on this fact take and benefit from his books. Certainly he produced works which were rare or unavailable that we were unable to acquire. Therefore it is necessary for the students of knowledge to write to him about this matter. And those who desire to refute him scholastically should do so. To Allaah alone we complain of many of the people today, how significantly they need to learn. How can this be? Because see that the early scholar Abu Haatim or Abu Zur'ah and other similar scholars have mentioned a hadeeth narration in their book ((al-'Ilal)04-14), then one of our companions today from the modern day verifiers of books says, [However, I say...] I say to him, who are you upon the scales of knowledge to come forth with [I say...]?!? Or they say, [In our view this impermissible.] Who are you to even have a view in this matter?!? And another such verifier says, [I differ with Imaam adh-Dhahabee.], or [I disagree with al-'Iraaqee.] or [I have a different opinion from as-Sakhaawee and Ibn Kaather.]! So if you differ with all of these leading scholars, then who stands with you upon your position?!

Such individuals need to gain deep understanding of and study the mentioned book ((al-'Ilal)04-14), which indicates the hidden defects in narrations. They are in need of understanding that there are only a limited number of scholars who specialize in this difficult branch of knowledge of hidden defects, such that you can count them upon your fingers. It is not simply anyone who has the ability to gain true competence in this field. One such verifier states, [I say, this addition to the narration is only narrated by such and such narrator but he is judged to be reliable and the addition to a narration of the reliable narrator is accepted.] But is the additional information from a reliable narrator always unconditionally accepted? Or is the proper position in fact that it is a condition that he does not contradict a narrator who is more reliable than him, and that it should be established that the early scholars who were masters of this specific branch of knowledge do not declare this specific narration of his to have a hidden defect?

*[FROM 'EXCELLENT RESPONSES TO QUESTIONS FROM THOSE PRESENT AND THOSE ABSENT': PAGE 118]*

# The Nakhlah Educational Series: Mission and Methodology (Pocket Edition)

## Mission

The Purpose of the 'Nakhlah Educational Series' is to contribute to the present knowledge based efforts which enable Muslim individuals, families, and communities to understand and learn Islaam and then to develop within and truly live Islaam. Our commitment and goal is to contribute beneficial publications and works that:

Firstly, reflect the priority, message and methodology of all the prophets and messengers sent to humanity, meaning that single revealed message which embodies the very purpose of life, and of human creation. As Allaah the Most High has said,

*We sent a Messenger to every nation ordering them that they should worship Allaah alone, obey Him and make their worship purely for Him, and that they should avoid everything worshipped besides Allaah. So from them there were those whom Allaah guided to His religion, and there were those who were unbelievers for whom misguidance was ordained. So travel through the land and see the destruction that befell those who denied the Messengers and disbelieved.*—(Surah an-Nahl: 36)

## Two Essential Foundations

Secondly, building upon the above foundation, our commitment is to contributing publications and works which reflect the inherited message and methodology of the acknowledged scholars of the many various branches of Sharee'ah knowledge who stood upon the straight path of preserved guidance in every century and time since the time of our Messenger, may Allaah's praise and salutations be upon him. These people of knowledge, who are the inheritors of the Final Messenger, have always adhered closely to the two revealed sources of guidance: the Book of Allaah and the Sunnah of the Messenger of Allaah- may Allaah's praise and salutations be upon him, upon the united consensus, standing with the body of guided Muslims in every century - preserving and transmitting the true religion generation after generation. Indeed the Messenger of Allaah, may Allaah's praise and salutations be upon him, informed us that, *{ A group of people amongst my Ummah will remain obedient to Allaah's orders. They will not be harmed by those who leave them nor by those who oppose them, until Allaah's command for the Last Day comes upon them while they remain on the right path. }* (Authentically narrated in Saheeh al-Bukhaaree).

The guiding scholar Sheikh Zayd al-Madkhalee, may Allaah protect him, stated in his writing, 'The Well Established Principles of the Way of the First Generations of Muslims: It's Enduring & Excellent Distinct Characteristics' that,

*"From among these principles and characteristics is that the methodology of tasfeeyah -or clarification, and tarbeeyah -or education and cultivation- is clearly affirmed and established as a true way coming from the first three generations of Islaam, and is something well known to the people of true merit from among them, as is concluded by considering all the related evidence. What is intended by tasfeeyah, when referring to it generally, is clarifying that which is the truth from that which is falsehood, what is goodness from that which is harmful and corrupt, and when referring to its specific meanings it is distinguishing the noble Sunnah of the Prophet and the people of the Sunnah from those innovated matters brought into the religion and the people who are supporters of such innovations.*

*As for what is intended by tarbeeyah, it is calling all of the creation to take on the manners and embrace the excellent character invited to by that guidance revealed to them by their*

*Lord through His worshiper and Messenger Muhammad, may Allaah's praise and salutations be upon him; so that they might have good character, manners, and behavior. As without this they cannot have a good life, nor can they put right their present condition or their final destination. And we seek refuge in Allaah from the evil of not being able to achieve that rectification."*

Thus the methodology of the people of standing upon the Prophet's Sunnah, and proceeding upon the 'way of the believers' in every century is reflected in a focus and concern with these two essential matters: tasfeeyah or clarification of what is original, revealed message from the Lord of all the worlds, and tarbeeyah or education and raising of ourselves, our families, and our communities, and our lands upon what has been distinguished to be that true message and path.

## Methodology:

*The Roles of the Scholars & General Muslims In Raising the New Generation*

The priority and focus of the 'Nakhlah Educational Series' is reflected within in the following statements of Sheikh al-Albaanee, may Allaah have mercy upon him:

*"As for the other obligation, then I intend by this the education of the young generation upon Islaam purified from all of those impurities we have mentioned, giving them a correct Islamic education from their very earliest years, without any influence of a foreign, disbelieving education."*

*(Silsilat al-Hadeeth ad-Da'eefah, Introduction page 2.)*

*"...And since the Messenger of Allaah, may Allaah's praise and salutations be upon him, has indicated that the only cure to remove this state of humiliation that we find ourselves entrenched within, is truly returning back to the religion. Then it is clearly*

*obligatory upon us - through the people of knowledge- to correctly and properly understand the religion in a way that conforms to the sources of the Book of Allaah and the Sunnah, and that we educate and raise a new virtuous, righteous generation upon this."*

*(Clarification and Cultivation and the Need of the Muslims for Them)*

It is essential in discussing our perspective upon this obligation of raising the new generation of Muslims, that we highlight and bring attention to a required pillar of these efforts as indicated by Sheikh al-Albaanee, may Allaah have mercy upon him, and others- in the golden words, "*through the people of knowledge*". Since something we commonly experience today is that many people have various incorrect understandings of the role that the scholars should have in the life of a Muslim, failing to understand the way in which they fulfill their position as the inheritors of the Messenger of Allaah, may Allaah's praise and salutations be upon him, and stand as those who preserve and enable us to practice the guidance of Islaam. Similarly the guiding scholar Sheikh 'Abdul-'Azeez Ibn Baaz, may Allaah have mercy upon him, also emphasized this same overall responsibility:

"*...It is also upon a Muslim that he struggles diligently in that which will place his worldly affairs in a good state, just as he must also strive in the correcting of his religious affairs and the affairs of his own family. As the people of his household have a significant right over him that he strive diligently in rectifying their affair and guiding them towards goodness, due to the statement of Allaah, the Most Exalted,* ◄ **Oh you who believe! Save yourselves and your families Hellfire whose fuel is men and stones** ► *-(Surah at-Tahreem: 6)*

So it is upon you to strive to correct the affairs of the members of your family. This includes your wife, your children- both male and female- and such as your own brothers. This concerns all of the people in your family, meaning you should strive to teach them the religion, guiding and directing them, and warning them from those matters Allaah has prohibited for us. Because you are the one who is responsible for them as shown in the statement of the Prophet, may Allaah's praise and salutations be upon him, **{ Every one of you is a guardian, and responsible for what is in his custody. The ruler is a guardian of his subjects and responsible for them; a husband is a guardian of his family and is responsible for it; a lady is a guardian of her husband's house and is responsible for it, and a servant is a guardian of his master's property and is responsible for it....}** Then the Messenger of Allaah, may Allaah's praise and salutations be upon him, continued to say, **{...so all of you are guardians and are responsible for those under your authority.}** (Authentically narrated in Saheeh al-Bukhaaree & Muslim)

It is upon us to strive diligently in correcting the affairs of the members of our families, from the aspect of purifying their sincerity of intention for Allaah's sake alone in all of their deeds, and ensuring that they truthfully believe in and follow the Messenger of Allaah, may Allaah's praise and salutations be upon him, their fulfilling the prayer and the other obligations which Allaah the Most Exalted has commanded for us, as well as from the direction of distancing them from everything which Allaah has prohibited.

It is upon every single man and women to give advice to their families about the fulfillment of what is obligatory upon them. Certainly, it is upon the woman as well as upon the man to perform this. In this way our homes become corrected and rectified in regard to the most important and essential matters. Allaah said to His Prophet, may Allaah's praise and salutations be upon him, ◈ **And enjoin the ritual prayers on your family...** ◈ (Surah Taha: 132) Similarly, Allaah the Most Exalted said to

*His prophet Ismaa'aeel,* ❧ *And mention in the Book, Ismaa'aeel. Verily, he was true to what he promised, and he was a Messenger, and a Prophet. And he used to enjoin on his family and his people the ritual prayers and the obligatory charity, and his Lord was pleased with him.* ❧ *-(Surah Maryam: 54-55)*

*As such, it is only proper that we model ourselves after the prophets and the best of people, and be concerned with the state of the members of our households. Do not be neglectful of them, oh worshipper of Allaah! Regardless of whether it is concerning your wife, your mother, father, grandfather, grandmother, your brothers, or your children; it is upon you to strive diligently in correcting their state and condition..."*

*(Collection of Various Rulings and Statements- Sheikh 'Abdul-'Azeez Ibn 'Abdullah Ibn Baaz, Vol. 6, page 47)*

**Content & Structure:**

We hope to contribute works which enable every striving Muslim who acknowledges the proper position of the scholars, to fulfill the recognized duty and obligation which lays upon each one of us to bring the light of Islaam into our own lives as individuals as well as into our homes and among our families. Towards this goal we are committed to developing educational publications and comprehensive educational curriculums -through cooperation with and based upon the works of the scholars of Islaam and the students of knowledge. Works which, with the assistance of Allaah, the Most High, we can utilize to educate and instruct ourselves, our families and our communities upon Islaam in both principle and practice. The publications and works of the Nakhlah Educational Series are divided into the following categories:

*Basic: Ages 4- 6*

*Elementary: Ages 6-11*

*Secondary: Ages 11-14*

*High School: Ages 14- Young Adult*

*General: Young Adult –Adult*

*Supplementary: All Ages*

Publications and works within these stated levels will, with the permission of Allaah, encompass different beneficial areas and subjects, and will be offered in every permissible form of media and medium. As certainly, as the guiding scholar Sheikh Saaleh Fauzaan al-Fauzaan, may Allaah preserve him, has stated,

*"Beneficial knowledge is itself divided into two categories. Firstly is that knowledge which is tremendous in its benefit, as it benefits in this world and continues to benefit in the Hereafter. This is religious Sharee'ah knowledge. And secondly, that which is limited and restricted to matters related to the life of this world, such as learning the processes of manufacturing various goods. This is a category of knowledge related specifically to worldly affairs.*

*...As for the learning of worldly knowledge, such as knowledge of manufacturing, then it is legislated upon us collectively to learn whatever the Muslims have a need for. Yet If they do not have a need for this knowledge, then learning it is a neutral matter upon the condition that it does not compete with or displace any areas of Sharee'ah knowledge..."*

*("Explanations of the Mistakes of Some Writers", Pages 10-12)*

We ask Allaah, the most High to bless us with success in contributing to the many efforts of our Muslim brothers and sisters committed to raising themselves as individuals and the next generation of our children upon that Islaam which Allaah has perfected and chosen for us, and which He has enabled the guided Muslims to proceed upon in each and every century. We ask him to forgive us, and forgive the Muslim men and the Muslim women, and to guide all the believers to everything He loves and is pleased with. The success is from Allaah, The Most High The Most Exalted, alone and all praise is due to Him.

*Abu Sukhailah Khalil Ibn-Abelahyi*
*Taalib al-Ilm Educational Resources*

BOOK PUBLICATION PREVIEW:

# *Al-Waajibaat:*
## *The Obligatory Matters*

**What it is Decreed that Every Male and Female Muslim Must Have Knowledge Of -from the statements of Sheikh al-Islaam Muhammad ibn 'Abdul-Wahaab**

(A Step By Step Course on The Fundamental Beliefs of Islaam- with Lesson Questions, Quizzes, & Exams)

*Collected and Arranged by*
*Umm Mujaahid Khadijah Bint Lacina*
*al-Amreekiyyah*

[Available: **Now - Self Study/ Teachers Edition**
price: (Soft cover) **$20** (Hard cover) **$27**
**Directed Study Edition** price: **$17.50** -
**Exercise Workbook** price: **$10** ¦ eBook **$9.99** ]

SCAN WITH SMARTPHONE

FOR MORE INFORMATION

SCAN WITH SMARTPHONE

FOR MORE INFORMATION

BOOK PUBLICATION PREVIEW:

# *Thalaathatu al-Usool: The Three Fundamental Principles*

A Step by Step Educational Course on Islaam
Based upon Commentaries of 'Thalaathatu al-Usool'
of Sheikh Muhammad ibn 'Abdul Wahaab
(may Allaah have mercy upon him)

*Collected and Arranged by Umm Mujaahid
Khadijah Bint Lacina al-Amreekiyyah*

## *Description:*

*A complete course for the Believing men and women
who want to learn their religion from the ground
up, building a firm foundation upon which to base
their actions. This is the* **second** *in our* **Foundation
Series** *on Islamic beliefs and making them a reality
in your life, which began with* **"al-Waajibaat: The
Obligatory Matters"***.*

[Available: **Now Self Study/ Teachers Edition** ¦
price: (Soft cover) **$22.50** (Hard cover) **$29.50**
**Directed Study Edition** price: (S) **$17.50** -
**Exercise Workbook** price: (S) **$10** ¦ eBook **$9.99**]

SCAN WITH SMARTPHONE     SCAN WITH SMARTPHONE

FOR MORE INFORMATION     FOR MORE INFORMATION

BOOK PUBLICATION PREVIEW:

*My Hijaab, My Path*

# A Comprehensive Knowledge Based Compilation on Muslim Women's Role & Dress

*Collected and Translated by*
*Umm Mujaahid Khadijah Bint Lacina*
*al-Amreekiyyah*

[Available: **Now**¦ pages: **190+** ¦ price: (S) **$17.50**
(H) **$25** ¦ eBook **$9.99**

SCAN WITH SMARTPHONE

PRINT

FOR MORE INFORMATION

SCAN WITH SMARTPHONE

EBOOK

FOR MORE INFORMATION

BOOK PUBLICATION PREVIEW:

# My Home, My Path

## A Comprehensive Source Book For Today's Muslim Woman Discussing Her Essential Role & Contribution To The Establishment of Islaam – Taken From The Words Of The People Of Knowledge

*Collected and Translated by*
*Umm Mujaahid Khadijah Bint Lacina*
*al-Amreekiyyah*

[Available: **Now** | pages: **420+** | price: (Soft cover) **$22.50** (Hard cover) **$29.50** (eBook) **$9.99**]

SCAN WITH SMARTPHONE

PRINT

FOR MORE INFORMATION

SCAN WITH SMARTPHONE

EBOOK

FOR MORE INFORMATION

BOOK PUBLICATION PREVIEW:

# *Fasting from Alif to Yaa:*

## *A Day by Day Guide to Making the Most of Ramadhaan*

-Contains additional points of benefit to teach one how to live Islaam as a way of life
-Plus, stories of the Prophets and Messengers including activities for the whole family to enjoy and benefit from for each day of Ramadhaan. Some of the Prophets and Messengers covered include Aadam, Ibraaheem, Lut, Yusuf, Sulaymaan, Shu'ayb, Moosa, Zakariyyah, Muhammad, and more! -Recipes for foods enjoyed by Muslims around the world

*By Umm Mujaahid Khadijah Bint Lacina al-Amreekiyyah as-Salafiyyah With Abu Hamzah Hudhaifah Ibn Khalil and Umm Usaamah Sukhailah Bint Khalil*

[Available: **1433** -pages: 250+ ¦ price: (S) **$20** (H) **$27** ¦ eBook **$9.99**

SCAN WITH SMARTPHONE

PRINT

FOR MORE INFORMATION

SCAN WITH SMARTPHONE

EBOOK

FOR MORE INFORMATION

BOOK PUBLICATION PREVIEW:

# The Cure, The Explanation, The Clear Affair, & The Brilliantly Distinct Signpost

*A Step by Step Educational Course on Islaam Based upon Commentaries of*

# 'Usul as-Sunnah' of Imaam Ahmad
(may Allaah have mercy upon him)

Study of text divided into chapters formatted into multiple short lessons to facilitate learning . Each lesson has: evidence summary, lesson benefits, standard & review exercises 'Usul as-Sunnah' Arabic text & translation divided for easier memorization.

*Compiled and Translated by:*
Abu Sukhailah Khalil Ibn-Abelahyi

[Available: **TBA** ¦ price: **TBA** (Multi-volume) ¦ soft cover, hard cover, ebook]

SCAN WITH SMARTPHONE

PRINT

FOR MORE INFORMATION

SCAN WITH SMARTPHONE

EBOOK

FOR MORE INFORMATION

BOOK PUBLICATION PREVIEW:

# *Whispers of Paradise (1): A Muslim Woman's Life Journal*

## An Islamic Daily Journal Which Encourages Reflection & Rectification

*Collected and Edited by Taalib al-Ilm Educational Resources Development Staff*

[Available: **Now** ¦ price: (Hard cover) **$32** ]
*[Elegantly designed edition is for the year 1434 / 2013]*

*12 Monthly calendar pages* with beneficial quotations from Ibn Qayyim
*Daily journal page* based upon Islamic calendar (with corresponding C.E. dates)

SCAN WITH SMARTPHONE

PRINT

FOR MORE INFORMATION

www.ingramcontent.com/pod-product-compliance
Lightning Source LLC
LaVergne TN
LVHW011219080426
835509LV00005B/209